HASTINGS CHILDHOODS

Hastings Modern History Workshop

Falmer
Centre for Continuing Education,
University of Sussex
1987

Front cover: All Saints Street. All Saints School, number 57, may just be seen on the right (the building with the pointed roof).

Published by the Centre for Continuing Education, University of Sussex
Printed by Delta Press
Typeset in Garamond by Oxford University Computing Service.

ISBN 0-904242-32-3

CONTENTS

PREFACE

Most people have very firm opinions about their childhood. Some look back with longing to carefree happy days. Others endured the experience, waiting to 'grow up', leave home and start work or a family. Some see their school days as the best days of their lives, while others look back on a loathsome experience they were delighted to see behind them.

Nowadays it is sometimes difficult to separate being a child from going to school. Since 1870 a complex education system built up in Britain that is controlled, in one way or another, by central and local government. In turn it usually has a huge impact on the daily lives and experiences of children. But the grandparents of some older people alive today had no formal education, or at best irregularly attended very inadequate schools.

This book is about both childhood and schools in Hastings. Part one is a series of personal accounts of people who were born in Hastings between 1897 and 1922. In these edited interviews people talk about their childhood experiences in the family and at home, school, play and work, and provide some graphic accounts of the town and its people in the first part of this century.

Part two covers a longer time span, from the early nineteenth century to 1945. It examines the development of schools and education in Hastings from a largely private and church dominated system to a far more comprehensive one, mostly managed and organised by Hastings Council itself, although under the sometimes strict guidance of central Government.

Part three complements the rest of the book, being a directory of schools in Hastings, particularly for the period from 1870 to 1945. As with part two, it is largely concerned with what today is known as the 'state sector'. It makes no attempt to provide a listing of the very large number of private fee-paying schools in the town, which were aimed at children of relatively well-off parents.

This book is the work of the Hastings Modern History Workshop. The Workshop began in 1979. One important dimension of its activities has been an annual series of weekly evening meetings organised by the University of Sussex, Centre for Continuing Education. It is largely at these meetings since October 1985 that the research for this book has been carried out. During 1986–7 the Workshop members were Fred Gray (the formal group leader and editor of this volume) Jean Donaldson, Ron Fellows, Ray Gladwish, Mike Greenhalgh, Jack Hodd, Relf Kenway, Pat Lambert, Brian Lawes, Brian Martin, Steve Peak, Colin Pope, Peter Rapley, and Mary Roberts.

Of those people working on childhood and schools in Hastings, Jack Hodd, Jean Donaldson, Mary Roberts and Pat Lambert were responsible for interviewing people about their childhoods. This material forms part one of the book. Part two, the history of education and schools in the town, is the result of the labours of Fred Gray, Jack Hodd, Mary Roberts, Ray Gladwish, Relf Kenway, Ron Fellows, and Steve Peak. For the schools directory (part three) Jean Donaldson, Mary Roberts and Pat Lambert studied the history of schools in the Old Town and central Hastings; Mike Greenhalgh and Relf Kenway looked at schools in St Leonards and west Hastings; and Brian Lawes, Colin Pope, Jack Hodd and Ray Gladwish examined schools in the remainder of the town including neighbourhoods such as Ore.

We are grateful to all the people who agreed to be interviewed and whose edited stories are reproduced in part one. In one or two cases, dates and the names of individuals and places have been changed to ensure anonymity.

Most of the regular evening meetings of the Workshop since the early 1980s have taken place in Hastings Reference Library at the Brassey Institute, Claremont. It is here that much of the research for this book has occured. We are grateful to all the library staff who have spent time making the Workshop work, but particularly wish to acknowledge the enthusiastic support of Pam Haines and Brion Purdey.

Workshop members have also drawn on the resources of Hastings Museum and the East Sussex Records Office, Lewes. Thanks especially to to Leslie Cornish and Graham Mayhew for their help, and for putting themselves out when they didn't need to.

Many of the illustrations come from the collections of individual Workshop members and from the pages of the Hastings and St Leonards Observer and Hastings and St Leonards Pictorial Advertiser. Thanks for other illustrations are due to Hastings Library, Hastings Museum, East Sussex Record Office, Mick Wales, and the individuals whose childhoods are recorded in part one.

Within the University of Sussex thanks are due to Cynthia Robson for word processing; Jane Carver, Karen Merrick, Morag Stalker and Sylvie Whittingdon for proof reading; Sheila Shardlow for fixing the typesetting; and Peter Morris for design and photographic advice and help.

Part One
Personal Accounts

INTRODUCTION

The following accounts are edited interviews of people talking about their lives as children in Hastings in the first two and three decades of the twentieth century.

Living and working in a seaside town has always been a precarious thing to do. Even in successful resorts, much work tends to be low paid and insecure. Resorts are also notorious for the ebb and flow of business and, in turn, jobs and residents. Fashions in places change—and tourists and wealthy residents come and go.

For much of the first four decades of this century Hastings people were in the unhappy position of living in a seaside town in decline. Wealthy visitors and residents were being attracted by the newer resorts of Eastbourne and Bexhill. The population of Hastings fell, while all other Sussex coastal towns increased in size. Many of the largest houses built for single families with servants were empty for long periods, eventually to be converted into flats.

The start of this period of decline is the time Robert Tressell lived and worked in Hastings and wrote 'The Ragged Trousered Philanthropists', a book which graphically describes many aspects of life, work and poverty in the town. But one of the limitations of Tressell's account is that it has little to say about children in Hastings, and their experiences of decline and poverty.

Although most of the people we spoke to do not have childhood memories going back to the first decade of the century, the evidence is that the situation in Hastings didn't begin to change for the better until the 1930s. From these accounts we can begin to build up a picture of life in Hastings and of the town itself at the time. Clearly, in some ways Hastings was exceptional. It was a seaside town, surrounded by countryside, and in decline. This situation had an impact on the experiences of children and is seen in the personal stories below, in family life, play, and work. On the other hand, Hastings people shared many common experiences with people from all over Britain—for example, the impact of the First World War, the inter-war economic crisis, the development of state education and the beginnings of the modern welfare state.

These eleven accounts show that poverty was a very common state of affairs. Even men in relatively high status and respectable occupations—such as the police force—had low incomes, and their wifes had a struggle to make ends meet. But some people were very much poorer than others. Sometimes this was because a breadwinner was out of work or absent. In a town like Hastings, service work—based on 'taking in each other's washing'—was often insecure and many adults had periods of umemployment. Several people whose childhood stories are reproduced here, lost a parent through death or family break-up. In other cases the work available was low paid and often very casual. It was sometimes paid in kind rather than cash. Getting a few fish for helping to pull a boat up the beach is one extreme example.

For the very poor, charity was often important, especially if children were to be fed, clothed and kept warm in winter. In Hastings there were boot funds, soup kitchens, and a number of other charities. But this sort of help was often inadequate. Some children were hungry for much of the time, and cold in the winter. Often people were forced through various hoops before they were able to receive help—attending chapel, church or Sunday school, being inspected and interviewed by charity officers, trying to catch the eye of people with tickets for free dinners, and so on. Indeed, the inadequacies of charity and pressures of poverty were such that during the decades from 1900, central and local government stepped in to provide an increasingly comprehensive welfare service for poor children if not adults—free school meals, medical help, and the like.

Another aspect of poverty that emerges from these accounts is the way in which both adults and children made use of what today would be thrown away. Poor people would buy, and painstakingly skin, the left over 'flaps' from prepared fish. Low quality or deteriorating food, such as broken fish or crystallised jam, was gratefully accepted. Although they were sometimes unhappy about it, children were often forced to wear ill-fitting passed down or cast-off clothes and shoes, for example at school and even special occasions such as May Day. Kitchen ranges were fuelled by anything that would burn including old boots. Jam jars and rags were sold by both children and adults and were an important way of getting a few extra pence. At worst people would

Enjoying the seaside—the Castle Rocks

4

Walter Wingrave (lay preacher, carpenter and undertaker) at one of his children's open-air beach meetings

scavenge amongst rubbish on the beach for cinders to burn.

Largely because of family poverty, most of the people we talked to had worked from a relatively young age. Even before leaving school most children had some form of part-time work, despite the fact that there were increasingly strict regulations issued by the Government and Hastings Council to try and control child employment. In some cases work clearly interferred with a child's schooling. It was often physically hard and time-consuming and on rare occasions even terrifying. But it was often a crucial supplement to a family's income.

Most children left school (and perhaps also their childhoods behind them) at fourteen. Girls typically went into service work as maids, laundry workers or shop assistants. Boys entered a wider range of occupations including building. No one went into what could be thought of as industry, and this reflects the nature of the employment opportunities available in a seaside town like Hastings.

Despite the often quoted saying about school days being the best days of your life, many of the people who spoke to us were quite happy or even thankful to have left school as soon as they could. In part this was because of the attractions of the outside world—especially the opportunity to get a regular income. But it was also because many children did not much like school—'blow school' as someone said.

Mount Pleasant Congregational School outing, August 1908

6

Sandown Mission Sunday School, February 1920

8

Children also often had a healthy disregard for the attempts of various other bodies and groups to influence them. Many went to Band of Hope meetings and Sunday school not because of the message but because of the opportunity to go on summer outings, to Christmas parties, or to keep out of the rain. And when there they were not always easy to control.

The following accounts also provide some unexpected insights into Hastings. We can begin to understand the important points in the town for children fifty or sixty years ago—the sweet shops, the street traders, the cinemas, the play places and the important role of the nearby countryside. Several people talk about the smells of the Old Town, most of which (perhaps thankfully) have long since been blown away. Some of the people we spoke to also lived in many different houses as children, usually moving within one neighbourhood, but sometimes going from say Ore to the Old Town, or even out of Hastings altogether. Most people rented their houses from private landlords—an unusual form of housing today—and this made moving about relatively easy, but some people were home owners.

Oral history is of considerable interest and value. Learning from people about their past experiences provides a much needed counter-balance to other approaches to history. We can start to appreciate what peoples' lives and the places they lived in were like at particular times. However, as with any of the approaches to looking at the past, oral history isn't without some difficulties. Each individual has different experiences and for a truly comprehensive picture we would need to attempt the impossible task of talking to everyone. Some people do not wish to be interviewed, or to answer particular questions. Sometimes there is no way of assessing the accuracy of what people say—memories may be faulty or people may wish to give an alternative impression about the past.

This should be bourne in mind in reading the following accounts of people's childhoods in Hastings. The eleven people included come from a relatively limited range of neighbourhoods and backgrounds. For example, we have not included anyone who had private schooling or who lived in the most affluent parts of Hastings. Another limitation is that some important aspects of childhood and adolescence are not touched upon. For example, we neither asked nor were often told much about first experiences of love and sex. When and how did people learn about 'the facts of life'? Were they told, or did they find out by trial and error? What happened about contraception?

Many of the people we talked to didn't have a lot to say about school. They could remember the names of some teachers and fellow pupils, and things like playground games and punishment by teachers. But most of them had little to say about what they were taught in the classroom. In general people were far happier talking about their childhood outside the school—whether this was about parents and family, housing, work, or play. And as the people we talked to were recalling their childhoods, there are obvious limitations to their perspectives on the schools they went to and on education in general. Most of the teachers, administrators and politicians of the period are long dead. Clearly, although oral history is a very important way of looking at the development of schools and education, it does need to be complimented, where possible, with other sources of information. For this reason, parts two and three of this book are largely based on written sources of information.

Further reading

More personal stories of life in Hastings before the Second World War (including other aspects of Alf Hodd's childhood) are to be found in the Hastings Modern History Workshop's 1982 book, *Hastings Voices* (HMHW and the Centre for Continuing Education, the University of Sussex). Personal accounts and autobiographies of childhoods in other places are contained in:

Bristol Broadsides (1983) *Bristol's Other History* (Bristol, Bristol Broadsides).

J. Burnett (1982) *Destiny Obscure.*

R. Roberts (1976) *A Ragged Schooling.*

J. Seabrook (1982) *Working-Class Childhood.*

See also the excellent QueenSpark Books about life in Brighton.

JANE ADES

Born 1897

I was born in Herstmonceaux and moved to Guestling when I was about five years of age. We lived down Guestling Lane in a little cottage until the First War, and then my father and mother moved up to Clifton Road. I went to three schools. I went to Guestling School and I went to Westfield School and I went to St Helens School. I used to live down Rock Lane and we used to have to go to St Helens. Where the High School is now. I had two brothers and two sisters.

My father was a builder. I don't remember him ever being out of work. While we was at Herstmonceaux he was a builder with his brother. The last bit of building my father done, he built Hellingly Asylum. And when he built that he told my mother he would never do another bit of building, so he moved to Guestling where he joined Mr Gooden, the farmer, milked the cows and that. We used to live in a little place down Guestling Road called Pigeoncote.

When she was sixteen my mother minded babies, she said, as big as herself, for a shilling a week. Later she worked in a laundry. She worked after she was married—my sisters were grown up and looked after us. My sister Lizzie, and Mary, were older. We used to play rounders and cricket at school. Football sometimes we did. And racing. There was a big field and I played with the other girls at the school.

I didn't do any jobs while I was at school, but we used to get a penny or two from our parents if we'd behaved ourselves. I remember one time my brother Arthur—he's younger than I am. He had a new pair of trousers on my mother had bought him, and he got on a tree and split them. Mother had been out shopping and we had a house with two steps. I was about eleven I think, so I said to Arthur 'I'll sew your trousers up'. He bent over and I was sewing when who should come along but my mother! She said 'What on earth are you doing?'. I said 'Arthur get up quick'. I said 'He's tore his trousers, I was trying to sew it up!'. 'I should think you would' she said. She was a bit cross but she had to laugh to think I was trying to do it before she came home.

You can guess what stitches it would be! Poor old Arthur and his new trousers.

I went to Sunday school at Westfield. My parents sometimes went to church. We used to go to Pett Level for our Sunday school outing in a bus. We used to be quite happy with that, plenty of seawater down there, there was.

My parents never took us on holidays. We used to go on school holidays and that, but that was one thing we never did. Occasionally we used to go to picnics—the farm where my father was they used to have a flower show up there—we used to go up there. Try to catch the greasy pig—they used to have a pig there grease all over. Greasy pole and all things like that. We used to go to those but never for holidays.

I left school when I was fourteen. I left on a Friday. On Saturday a lady called at my mother's house and she said 'I hear your daughter's left school'. My mother said 'Yes'. She said 'I want a kitchen maid. Do you think you could send her to me?'. You didn't have to say no like they do today. My mother said 'Oh, yes, she'll come'. So on the Monday I was a kitchen maid. I lived in. Started work at six o'clock in the morning until ten o'clock at night. What I didn't have to do! I don't think I ever shed so many tears in my life. They brought me goose—geese and chicken—I had to pick all them. I said to the cook, 'I can't do all that'. 'You got to do 'em. You're my kitchen maid!' I could

The High School

do 'em now. I could do 'em after. But I didn't know I'd have to do all those. And I was only fourteen.

I got half a crown a week and my off duties was four to eight o'clock and ten to one Sundays so I could go to church. There was ladies' maids then—two housemaids, parlourmaids and lady's maid. I used to go through the lady's maid's room to my room, and she had a bell like the town crier had, and at six o'clock to get me awake to do the old grates, she used to ring that. I used to hear that all right! So I got up in time to do the fire all nice and hot so the cook could cook the lady's dinner. They didn't have gas and that in those days. They learnt me to do everything—it hasn't hurt me.

I had long hair and I had to have it all done up in a bun and wear a mob cap. They said they didn't want no hairs in the food! We used to wear print frocks in the morning with a little collar, and you had to dress in black in the afternoon with a little short apron. We was proper skivvies—servants.

I didn't give my mother any money then. I think I spent it on things like sweets. I was only fourteen. My mother did say once 'You know my girl, you're not always going to have that money'. I used to give her some when I got older.

I think I was there about ten years. After that my people moved to Clifton Road, Ore, and I went too, and was a parlour maid with my friend. I was never out of work. I was there several years. Then I came back when my people died. And then I went as cook to Mount Pleasant Hospital. I was there about twenty years.

ELSIE VENESS

Born 1902

I was born at the Old Town Police Station where we lived for nearly
thirty years. Then we moved into the Croft when Mother died, and
from there I went to St Leonards to start my married life. I had three
brothers and two sisters. I was the fourth one down, there was two
brothers after me.

When George was born, Mother had old Granny White of Old
Town. Mother was forty-two when he was born, and she'd gone about
five years. Granny White said she'd better have a doctor because of her
age. So we had Dr. Baker and he lived at Old Hastings House. It was
ten and sixpence for the delivery. I went into the bedroom and Mother
was walking round with the pain. They sent me out saying she would
be better soon. My sister Mabel was seventeen years old and she came
home to look after us. But Dad wasn't helpless in the home. Next
morning he told us we'd got this new baby. We never had cots, the
baby slept in the feather bed with Mother and Father.

When I was born my father was twenty-eight. He was a policeman.
Before that he was in the tar yards at Maidstone where he was a
foreman. When he joined the police force he tossed up between
Hastings or the Metropolitan and he came down Hastings, and that's
how we came to Hastings. My eldest brothers and sister were born in
Maidstone, but us other four were Sussex Old Towners. Mother came
from Sevenoaks. She was a children's nurse not a registered nanny, but
from Sevenoaks she went to Maidstone and met my father.

Directly she was married the babies started coming along. She had
six and never went out to work, though she was a female searcher.
They wanted her to accompany a female prisoner to Lewes or
Maidstone where they were sent, but she went in front of the Watch
Committee and said she couldn't do it as she had four young children
and no relations in Hastings to give eye to them. That is when they
introduced a matron to the Central Police Station, and her husband. Mr
and Mrs Pain. He was a baker. He sold the business and he went as
town hall messenger and Mrs Pain done the female searching.

My mother used to get a shilling for each prisoner for searching them. She'd have a customer, and she would only have a whistle and she was only a little woman. She'd do it in the cells.

There was a pawn shop in George Street and they'd have a customer come and pawn some nice stuff. Then they'd ring up the police station and say 'What have you got on your list of stolen goods, have you got so and so, as so and so has just brought it in'. Then they'd tell where she lived (it was mostly women) and the police would go to that address and bring them down and my mother would search them. They would know my mother as Mrs Roberts. They would say 'I must go to the lavatory first', and Mother used to say 'Oh, we will get this over with first, then you can go'. They would say 'Oh I can't', and Mother would say 'Oh yes you can'. But the idea of it was they wanted to get to the toilet to put the pledge ticket down the lav.

Up the back of our house was the sixpenny doss house and it was run by the Italians. There was one little pub up there. It was run by Carrie Orsai and her husband Andy Orsai. Hop picking time that used to be packed because the people that had the doss house had extra money. They used to buy the kids things but it was mostly spent on drink. Then there'd be a flare up, there'd be fighting and stabbing, then there'd be two inside. Sometimes old John Epton, from the pub what was near our Police Station, said 'No more Phoebe you've had quite enough'. He wouldn't serve her and she come out and stood there (course she was Irish) swearing. She said 'Take that', and she put her elbow through the window doors. He come out and across to the station to whoever was on duty. She was fined half a crown—she wasn't locked up for that. And the men used to up with their knives or give their wives a good beating. We were brought up with that. I used to enjoy a good fight.

We felt we were ordinary working class. Our policemen were more looked up to than today. In the Old Town there was the sixpenny doss house, that breed. They were Italians and Irish. They were the lowest. Then came the fishermen, they were the next best. Of course they were very poor. Through the winter they used to knock at my mother's back door to ask if she'd got any boots for them, and time we'd finished with them, the boot laces were the only things any good. Next door to where we lived they had maids. The Italians up until the 1914 War always wore Italian clothes, one girl used to go with her father and dance to the organ. Harry Mamonne used to sell hot chestnuts and potatoes in George Street. In the summer he sold ice cream. Maggie Martino hung herself up by the doss house and my father had to cut her down. Then there was the little business people. We came in that category. There was certain people in Old Town they knew us and they'd play but they would never ask us to play with them. In High Street they were all business people. If I knew there was certain people in Stangers I wouldn't buy two halfpenny candles in front of them.

I went to Waterloo Council School in the Bourne. Some of the finest brains came out of that school. People I knew grew up to hold good jobs in the town—the building society, the managers, school teachers. Miss Shuttleworth was the head governess, she lived in Milward Road. We started at three and at six the girls went upstairs but the boys went to Clive Vale or Priory Road. My two brothers went to Priory Road. We used to look through the railings of Priory Road and watch the two boys playing there.

I liked my school teachers but one of them didn't like me. Miss Beeching she to come for me in drill. She'd call the other girls by their Christian names but she always called me Elsie Roberts. In the end my father wrote her a note 'Will you come and see me if you have a complaint against my daughter and I'll put it right, but if you don't stop molesting her I'll put a blue paper in your hand'. She wasn't nice to me after that, but she did stop going for me. We used to get the rule, I was a bit messy in my books and used to wipe the pen on my pinafore. I was top of the class for acting, geography, history and religion. I left school at fourteen. I wouldn't have liked to have stayed on longer.

We used to go to cookery lessons at Mount Pleasant School. Perhaps we'd make a cottage pie or a pudding. The school found the ingredients. It was all miniature, each girl done it small and if you wanted to buy it it used to be a penny or halfpenny. One thing we used to say was 'We haven't any money Miss, can we pay you next week?', and she'd say 'Yes', and put it in a book, and time we'd got home we'd eaten it. We had nothing to show our mothers. The next week we would take the money. If the girls really couldn't afford the money I don't know what they did with the food. They was little china dishes and you took the dishes back or if she felt nasty you would have it in a bit of paper.

Elsie

There was twenty girls in a class. Every now and then we'd have a nurse come and look at our hair and if you got nits or lice which a lot of us had, the nurse would put it down and the next day there would be a bottle of kaolin to take home. It was the most embarrassing thing of my life, and I was only a little girl, that I had a bottle of that to take home to my mother to clean my head. Terrible it was. They never seemed to keep all heads clean. There was clean heads, but before long they had the lice in there. I used to sit at the desk with some real poor people, poor and ignorant, and you'd see the lice going up their hair. It was ignorance apart from poorness.

We had long hair. My mother used to take us to old Mr Shipman, a chemist in High Street. He was a poor man's doctor really, because you had to pay the doctor. My mother told Mr Shipman 'Can you do anything with this child's hair?' I hadn't got lice, but I'd got nits, they're babies for lice, and he said 'Oh yes, I'll give you something', and he gave us some powder, 'pecifitic powder'. She put it in a tin with some lard in it, put it in the oven to melt, and then mixed it and rubbed it in. We got rid of them. Then I still had them, and he said 'There's only one thing to do here and that is to have her shorn because she breeds them'. I worried my mother to death. To go to bed at night I had to wear my father's ceremonial gloves to stop me scratching. I can't tell you when it started to clear up. My other sisters never had it—it was just me. When they said about being shorn, what a disgrace to go to school in the class and be cut, because the only girls to be cut was the gyppos or the poor people of the doss house when they was lousy. My mother used to do our hair night and morning. She used to kaolin it and go through it with a small tooth comb. I've heard her say 'I wish all you girls were boys. I don't have it with the boys'.

We had all very mixed people in our school. Some girls dressed like little princesses—beautiful—I used to envy them their lovely embroidered pinafores and ribbons. Then there was us, the class that was clean but not highly dressed. We had pinafores but not embroidered. Then there was gyppos, pikies, lodging house crew as we called them, and some very poor people. One family had three girls, Faith, Hope and Charity, who lived in the little cottage back of our police station. The old Grandmother used to sit outside and smoke her clay pipe. Now they were the type that would stop at nothing. Well they were in our class at school.

You didn't have individual trays in those days. You had one tray and teacher did all the modelling of mountains and rivers and that. She took her rings off and used to say 'Elsie Roberts, I want you out here to wear these rings'. She said 'You go right to the top of that class up in the corner out of everybody's way', because she had her handbag and a desk with stuff in, and she couldn't trust that with the type of some of the girls we had. So of course I did that, not because I was the best one but because I happened to live in the police station. I very often say an address is influential.

I was about seventeen or eighteen and in those days I worked at 52 Robertson Street, the Lane's sweet shop. He had lots of shops He lived at Wykeham Road. In those days you had no dinner hour, it was a recognised thing. But the government bought in the law that everybody should have an hour for dinner, and so Father said 'If you can get home within an hour and have a hot dinner you can do so'. I could walk it because it wasn't far from Robertson Street to Courthouse Street. One day the governor came in, Mr Lane, and there was lots of goods on the floor and it was mid-day and they should have been put away so he said 'What about all these goods, Miss?' to the manageress. So she said, 'Well they were late in delivering', so he said 'Where's the girl?' which was me. She said 'She's gone home to dinner'. 'Gone home to dinner Miss?'. How long has this been going on?'. She said 'The law's come in which they must have an hour's dinner now'. He said 'Where does she live?' 'In Old Town'. Well that finished it. I was a peasant because I came from Old Town. He said 'Well, you've got a gas ring haven't you?' So she said 'Oh yes, but her father said if she can get home in that hour she's to do so. Her father's a policeman, she lives at the police station'. I can see him now. He said 'Well Miss, if you can manage you'd better do it hadn't you'. Because I lived at the police station he never said any more and I had my hour.

Four or five shillings was a lot of money to take home in those days. I had ninepence or one shilling pocket money. I used to start at eight in the morning and work until eight in the evening and nine to twelve on Saturdays and all holidays for five shillings a week. We got no extra money, not even a bar of chocolate. The manageress was there for years and years. She went there at nine and came out at eight every night. She brought her food and cooked it on the gas ring downstairs where all the mice were. Full of mice it was. When I was at Plummer Roddis in the counting house being taught to be a ledger clerk, I got three shillings. That was when Lloyd George brought in the National Health and that was three pence so I had ninepence for my pocket money and threepence for the insurance, and I gave my mother two shillings to keep me and dress me. Police pay was very poor you know.

At the police station our living rooms and our bedrooms was all upstairs. There was four bedrooms. Three were over the cells and the other one was over the lower kitchen where Mother did all her washing and that. It was a beautiful place. Our sitting room was over the office of the police station and entrance. It was all on our own and the cells was downstairs and then there was a long corridor where Father used to keep all his uniform, and it was heavy uniform in those days you know. The winter coats, well I couldn't lift 'em. They weren't big rooms, only the kitchen and our living room. That was a big room because it was the same size as the fire station downstairs. When they practised there Tuesday or Thursday night, the row they made. Anybody coming in they used to think whatever's that row, and Mother used to say 'That's the men talking'. We got used to it of course. The firemen didn't live on the premises. They had to come from home and they all had the firebells in their homes. The policemen held the keys to the front of the fire station. He had to open the door for them to bring the hose out. Course it was all horses.

My mother used to do all her own work, and she had to take her washing on the beach to dry. Us girls we had to take four props and the lines. We were the advance guard. We'd take it down there and the fisherman that knew Mother would put up the line for her from the old capstan to another capstan. Then where you put the two props up they would put a lot of big boulders, or the wind would take it away. Then my mother would follow with a big basket and she'd carry it on her hip. Because my brothers were all big their shirts were all big. Then when they were all dry, she'd go down and gather them all in. Us children, when we come back from school, would bring the props and line in. They was all kept in our big kitchen downstairs with the dustbin and that sort of thing. Mother had it all to do. She was dead at fifty-three.

My dad would help in the house. He'd always clean the knives. We only had the old brick dust and the boards. He was a good gardener. He had two allotments so that we should have fresh vegetables because we had no garden or anything. He had one in Halton and one in Clive Vale, where there's the Roman Catholic School playground now. He used to grow potatoes at one and vegetables at the other. He used to pay tuppence for a handcart to bring all the stuff down with the boys.

The gyppos round at the sixpenny doss house, Sunday morning you'd see them go down with their baking tins with their potatoes and their roast beef on top. They'd take it to Mr Cramp (his son was the head one at the building society, and his daughter was one of our teachers). He used to bake it and charge a penny. Then they'd go about half past twelve and bring it home. Well they had a big oven up there but it would have to be done separately, but he could bake it when he baked his loaves.

We never done anything like that. In our living room we had a kitchener. My father would use that even in the summer time. My mother would have a fire for the cooking and perhaps she'd lay the tea in the front room because it would be cooler in there. But we never had gas or anything like that. When I was a girl, Mother only had a lamp and when we went to bed we had to go by candles. Afterwards she had gas put on in the living room; but a friend of ours put it on. Then we had a little lamp on the landing, and that was taken to Mother's bedroom. They slept with that all night in case one of us woke up. There was no switching on lights, and by the time you found matches and that, if Father was called out, it was too long.

You see we used to have some rough customers there, and he'd get up in the night if they kept banging the lavatory seats, and the policeman downstairs wouldn't go and quieten them. Father's gone down many a time and said, 'I'm going to shut him up', and the policeman would say 'Oh they'll be all right'. But Father said 'Your wife's sleeping all right, my wife and children can't sleep with the banging'. He'd go in there and take their boots off and take them away, and he said 'If you keep banging that lavatory seat up and down, I'll chain you to that post and you won't move'. It was only drink that done it and in the early hours when they had sobered up a bit and they was scared of Father because they knew they would get a clout off of him. Whether he ever did or not I don't know. They was scared of him. He was their friend and he was their enemy.

Through the 1914 war, Father was on duty there. The women whose husbands or men had gone had got to put in for their pension or their allowance. They couldn't spell their names and they'd come down and say 'Will you spell this for me Mr. Roberts?'. Some wasn't even married and, when they come home used to slip off to the Register Office and get married. It was no disgrace for them people, because

P.C. Roberts with two detectives outside the Old Town Police Station

they was very loyal to one another. But in the war they couldn't have got their money without being married.

Many a time my father would pay for a tramp to stay in the doss house. He used to have so many tickets to give to people as an entrance fee to the workhouse. 'Take this and give it to Mary Ann and tell her Mr. Roberts will pay for you in the morning'. My father was never out of work, but in the 1914 war the London police went on strike, and they won the day and the police pay went up by leaps and bounds. My father was conscious of taking it because they (the strikers) all got the sack.

At eight o'clock us children had to clear up, and Mother used to say 'There goes the curfew time for bed'. No sooner she got us to bed than she'd have to get Father a meal when he come in off late duty. She'd sit down after tea perhaps at six with her paper and we'd take her hair down and do it all up, make out we was hairdressers and that kind of thing. If Father was at home he would sit and read a good book or get the Police Review with sums in to do. Mother would get up on her nursing chair and brush him down. I can see him now folding his cape up. When he was wearing his big coat, he would put his handcuffs in his trouser pocket with one just hanging outside. His truncheon was in the long back pocket, his whistle was poked in his top pocket, and he carried his caddy tin with his tea in, and he'd put his sandwiches in the big pockets they had. The last thing he'd do would be to put his tobacco pouch in his trousers and his pipe, because after twelve o'clock they could smoke.

When we were little children Saturday nights, Father would be on night duty till half past nine. Mum would bath us in front of the kitchen fire. But in later years when we went out to work, with the boys particularly, down in the lower kitchen Mother used to light the copper. It was lovely down there. She'd have a cottage bath and the boys would go down there. Us girls didn't as things got better. We used to go down the baths which was only at the bottom of the road. Mr. Dunk was the man. If you took your own towel it was threepence. If he gave you a towel it was sixpence. You'd have your bath, then there'd be a knock on the door 'Come on it's time you were out'.

I used to have a Friday halfpenny for pocket money from Mum and a halfpenny from Dad. I spent it on a farthing's worth of tiger nuts. We used to go in Stricklands and buy Locusts. They never gave you a paper bag, you had to put it in your pinafore pocket. It had big pips and a kind of honey in it. We used to take it on the beach and eat it. Then we'd go up the Bourne to Mrs. Hudson and buy a farthing's worth of scorched peas or everlasting strip or hanky panky. That was pink white pink very fine nougat. I don't suppose it weighed more than half an ounce. Tiger nuts, scorched peas hard or soft, and aniseed balls, they was a hundred for a penny.

If we had a birthday my mother would go down to Avery's which was a shop in George Street and buy a sixpence halfpenny doll, and she'd dress it very amateurish. She could darn and mend, but she was no maker, but anyway we was pleased with it. We may have had a friend in to tea. She'd make a cake and put a clean tablecloth on but that was about all, birthdays weren't celebrated. We had lovely Christmases though. My mother would say to Floss and I about Christmas coming and she'd make the Christmas puddings and we'd always have a taster. In those days she had peel that had crystallised sugar in it, and she'd chop it on the suet board, and right at the corner would be three pieces for us girls to eat.

At Christmas Father used to go down to a place in York Buildings. I think it's a chemists now, but it was a big fruiterers then. Pollits the name was, and Christmas Eve if Father was off he'd take a sack, a small sack. I've seen him come home with nuts, apples and oranges and medlars. And a coconut and carry it on his shoulders where he carried his police cape. He always walked in the gutter never on the path because he was a big man. That went straight into my mother's wardrobe until Christmas Day, then it was all laid out. Us children had Taragona port wine to drink, it was two and sixpence for a quart bottle. We used to go over to Stangers, which is still there today, to buy that. They had wine I think. We had a big round table in our sitting room which was all laid out directly after dinner. Even the jellies and blancmanges was put out, with the fruit and nuts, and you helped yourself. He always cracked mother a Brazil and he always smoked a cigar. He had a carver in the kitchen which he took into the front room. That was his favourite chair.

My mother used to play the piano, and us girls had to learn a little ditty and we had to act it and sing it on Christmas night. John and Norman Epton would come over from the pub opposite and have a drink and we'd dance and mimic and we'd keep that up until two o'clock in the morning. We'd have a Christmas stocking, an ordinary black stocking. My grandmother would send us girls a knitted Peter Pan collar. The boys would have a box of chocolate soldiers. Then Mother would buy us an extra nice pinafore.

We never had a fowl, not working class people. We either had a aitch bone or perhaps a leg of pork. They were quite reasonable. With a leg of pork you could cut and come again with six of us in the family and the boys were quite big eaters and so was Father.

When I was about ten the Beavises, whose grandfather was a fisherman, went to the Winkle Club Christmas Dinner. You never went by ticket. Whoever was there first got in and there was a pushing and a shoving — it's a wonder no-one got killed. The ones I remember was in the Institute in All Saints Street, the Fishermen's Institute now. The big hall at the top. All the women used to do all the cooking, but Mr. Cramp the baker did all the baking, all the rolls and all the cakes. I went to one, Old Glad Beavis said 'You hang on to me Else, I'll get you in', and we were pushing and shoving and she got me in. But after that each individual had so many tickets, you went by ticket when it got so big. Mr. Dobson who was caretaker of the chapel, Mr. Kenward

Waiting for the Winkle Club Christmas Dinner 1912

he'd have so many tickets, the police would have so many, the business men who gave the stuff would have so many. I know father said he had half a dozen tickets and I said 'Oh, Dad, can I have one?'. He said 'No, there's poorer children than you want it'. He wouldn't give it to us. He give it to poorer children because there was a lot of poverty in Old Town with the fishermen, because they would go weeks and weeks, and couldn't get off the beach.

There was no money. That's where the pawn brokers came in. All their things went into the pawnshop. Even the sheets off the bed went there, because I went with a girl once, I'll never forget it. She said 'I'm going down to shop to take this pair of sheets are you coming?'. So she went into the passage by Wrights, not through the main shop, and she put the sheets up there and I think she got half a crown. He gave a ticket, the name and address. If it was there more than a fortnight you'd got to pay interest, but if you got it back within the fortnight you'd just put your half crown and get it back. I went home to my mother and told her I'd been with Lizzie Moon down the shop and sold a pair of sheets for two and sixpence. When I told her where I'd been she nearly had a fit. She said 'You mustn't go there'. I said 'Why not?'. She said 'That's the pawn shop'. Well I didn't know what a pawn shop meant, but if it had got round Mrs. Roberts pawns sheets, and we had to set an example in Old Town. If we done anything wrong we had a good hiding when we got home because we was a disgrace to the police station. Opposite was Stratfords. That was a pawn shop. In time you'd see sheets, pillow cases, counterpanes and that outside all for sale, that people had pawned and couldn't come back for.

On Sunday when we were young children we went to a little place in the Bourne, the Bourne Mission. Well at ten thirty in the morning it was finished, and we didn't know what to do, so we went for a walk in the park. So my father thought we ought to go to Sunday school, so that when it was wet we could go straight into chapel. That got us out of Mother's way until twelve o'clock. So from the Bourne Mission we went up to the Ebenezer. If it was wet we had to go straight into chapel, but when it was fine we went through the park of up to the cemetery. The Beavises and us. We had to walk nicely, no fooling about. Then in the afternoon we went to Sunday school. In the evening, if it was wet, or we didn't know what to do, we went across to our own chapel next door. Three times a day we had it until we were fourteen, then when we went out to work Father didn't make us go.

From the time we were three to fourteen we had to go. All the boys had to go to Sunday school morning and afternoon and chapel in the evening. My father would have no frivolities indoors on a Sunday. And my mother wasn't allowed to buy a pennorth of anything. If she forgot, say a packet of gravy thickening and father would be on duty downstairs, when we came from Sunday school, Mother used to say 'Go up to Mr. Kent (that was a little shop in All Saints Street) and get this packet of gravy thickening, but don't go in the front door—go at the back up the Creek Steps, so Father won't see it'. If not there would have been hell's delight to think we'd gone shopping on a Sunday.

In the summer we had our outings. We went by train to Battle or Pevensey or Rye. We all met at Sunday school and marched down to the railway station. If we got there early in the queue we got the window seat. To have the window seat was something marvellous. We usually used to have about ninepence each. Now that took a lot of time to get with four of us going. Very often my mother would get some rags she'd think was no good, and we'd take them up to old Verrells in the Bourne and we'd get some money for them. Or jam jars. I've known her take the jam out of the jar and put it into a basin, wash it and sell it for us children to have pocket money to take on our outings. We always bought her a penny bunch of roses from one of the little old houses, because she loved flowers and we had no garden.

In the winter we had our treat at the Public Hall over where Smiths is now. We had a tea with trestle tables. We always took our own mug and there was always a garment for each child: a petticoat, pair of knickers, a vest, even to a liberty bodice or a pair of stockings. Then there was a big thick tree with a small present for you. The boys used to have a small box of soldiers. At the top of the tree was a fairy, always a fairy, and the best girl of the class used to get that. I had it once, just once. I treasured it. Working class people never had trees, only the middle classes did.

As a child I played with anyone and everyone. I used to go up round the lodging house. There was one little girl there who was humpty-backed. Her name was Norah Sullivan, and her sister was Becky. Her father sold flowers, he used to carry them in a basket on his head. They only had two little rooms, but her mother kept her nice and if I could get with her I was everybody. I had nice school friends, but outside of school if there was a dirty girl or a poor girl I was there. The children always got on well with my father. We played basket ball at school and

PC Roberts, 'the Soup Constable', distributing soup kitchen tickets February 1910

I was captain, not that I was a good player but I was tough and I always come out top at acting and geography and all those things because nothing frightened me.

We wasn't supposed to get dirty when we played because we hadn't got a second lot of clothes to put on. We went to school Monday mornings with a clean starched and ironed pinafore and that afternoon we had to play basket ball. If it was not pouring hard but wet you can imagine the state we got in because we didn't have sports clothes. Mother used to come in and say 'Why can't your teacher have basket ball on Fridays when your school days are finished and it doesn't matter if you get dirty?'.

We played marbles and diablo and it was all boys and girls playing outside the police station and the hoops and tops on a string. We couldn't afford the twopence for the diablo, we used to use the reels off the tacking cotton, take the poker and burn it to make a groove to put the fine string round. That was our diablo. We always had a hoop, and May garland day my mother used to dress all our hoops up with flowers out of her window box, or we'd go up to get buttercups and daisies from Tarry High field and she'd tie them on with cotton. We had our own names for things in Old Town. We used to play leap frog. Easter we used to go up on the West Hill and we used to play skips. We had our hot cross buns, that was four skips, two girls stood opposite each other and another two girls opposite the other way, with skipping ropes to represent the cross, and you had to skip between them, that was called cross lines, but it was to represent hot cross buns.

When we had our summer holidays, we used to go over to Fairlight Glen or Ecclesbourne Glen the whole of the day. Our mother would give us our food, bits of chocolate or broken biscuits. Then the next day we would go on the beach all day, we'd go there at nine and stop there until nine at night. My mother found out we'd been in the water because her washing water went hard with the salt in our petticoats. We never had bathing costumes or anything like that. We were restricted from playing skipping games and games that meant kneeling because we wore the toes of our shoes out and my father couldn't afford to always be buying new ones.

We always wore boots. They was heavy to protect our ankles. A woman came round to Mother and she was running a club. Mother asked her what she was selling. She said mostly children's clothing. 'Do you sell boots?'. She said 'Yes'. You must remember that a pair of boots or shoes only cost two and elevenpence or three and elevenpence. 'Bring round a pair of boots for my young Else'. Course I was a rough one. She bought a pair of button shoes with white eyelets up to the ankle. They was a kind of polished leather, not patent, I said 'Can I have them?'. Well we had them. Sunday morning was a ritual getting ready for Sunday school, with fur coat and fur hat and a piece of chiffon. Our brothers had a bit of blue ribbon on their collars and off we went. When Father saw them he said 'What boots has she got on then?'. So mother said new ones. He said 'What has she got those new fangled things for? Ruin her feet'. Mother said 'Oh no it won't'. But she never told him she had them on the club. Mother had several things after that, she wanted us to have something dainty but she had to do it unbeknown to Dad. If he knew she owed money, oooh. In those days there was no overtime if the police did extra time. If they went into court for two hours you got four hours off.

My mother even did a bit of summer letting unknown to the authorities, to buy our winter coats. She let to friends from London, some came from when Father was on duty at the Memorial, they would ask him if he knew of anywhere for lodgings.

TOM GASSON

Born 1903

I was born on October 12th 1903 in 2 Mulberry Cottages in the Old Town, behind the St Mary Star-of-the-Sea Church that is now. I presume it was called that because there was a big mulberry tree there at the bottom of Douches Passage at All Saints Street. You came down the back there into the Bourne. I did sample some of those mulberries when I was a bit older. I don't know who the tenant of that house was—it may have been my grandparents or Mother may have rented a room from a friend. She used to say that her friend May Fuller used to take me out in the pram when we lived there. My father was in South Africa. He'd taken a discharge from the Boer War, but he had gone back, and was working as a coachman to a judge. My sister Dorian can remember Mother saying that when she answered a knock on the door one day it was Dad standing there, like a scarecrow. He'd worked his passage home from South Africa.

After that I lived with my mother and maternal grandparents at the bottom of Waterloo Passage. Granny looked after me while Mother went back into service. I'm not sure if she lived in, but I do have memories of being dressed in a sailor suit and toddling down the Bourne to meet her sometimes—perhaps on her day off. I can remember her taking me up Torfield, Tarry High field as we used to call it then. Once I remember her taking me to a house where she worked in Holmesdale Gardens and the lady of the house gave me a cake. I remember it because she opened a drawer and there was a plate of cakes in the drawer! The lady was called Mrs La Touche. At a later date Mrs La Touche moved to the house in Wykeham Road right at the top of the steps and Mum took me there too.

My grandparents had a house just opposite the pump in the Bourne. Later on they lived in All Saints Place at the bottom of Ebenezer Road and one of my first memories is of Grandad boiling a kettle on an oil stove—a double burner it was—called a 'Beatrice'. He made tea and toast. He always cut the crust off the toast and put it in with his tea. I can remember Gran making a gurnard pie, an open one, and coming down on the beach with Grandad. When I was a little older he came one day with a basket of blackberries which he said that he had got over the Govers. I think that was at Fairlight.

I went to the Waterloo School while living with Granny Adams, but my only memory of it is missing a school treat because I had whooping cough and the teacher sent me up some goodies. I would have been three or four at that time.

When Dad came back from South Africa we moved up to Hardwicke Road. I remember trying to tear a piece of cloth with my teeth and pulling four of them out!

The first time I went hopping was when we were living at Hardwicke Road. My mother and father hired a bedroom in the village and I remember one night when I got into bed—I was sleeping at one end and my mother and father at the other end—the leg of the bed went straight through the floor and the ceiling of the downstairs room. Then we went up to the High Bank at Ore. There must have been an election about that time because I stood on the High Bank watching the horses and carriages going down and the coachmen had flags and rosettes on their whips.

My father's parents Granny and Grandad Gasson, lived at 9 School Road, Ore, and on summer evenings—this would have been the weekend more, I suppose, we used to go down there, because Granny had a harmonium and Grandad had a kind of musical box—it wasn't a gramophone but you had to turn a handle. There were sheets of music that slipped in and when you turned the handle it played the music. Mum had a good voice and there was always one song Grandad wanted. You see he came from Folkestone and there were a couple of girls murdered there sometime or other, and this song was about them. Mum hated that song about the two girls, Caroline and Maria—it was supposed to be true. It started off 'Early one morning, before the break of day' and went on something like 'all young girls take warning'. I don't remember all the words. I always used to blub when she sang it— she hated singing it and I didn't like hearing it. Aunt Flora used to play the organ and we used to sing 'When the mists have rolled away'. I liked that one. We sang all those old hymns and songs. I was the only one in the family then so they could go out on a Saturday and take me with them.

Grandfather Adams

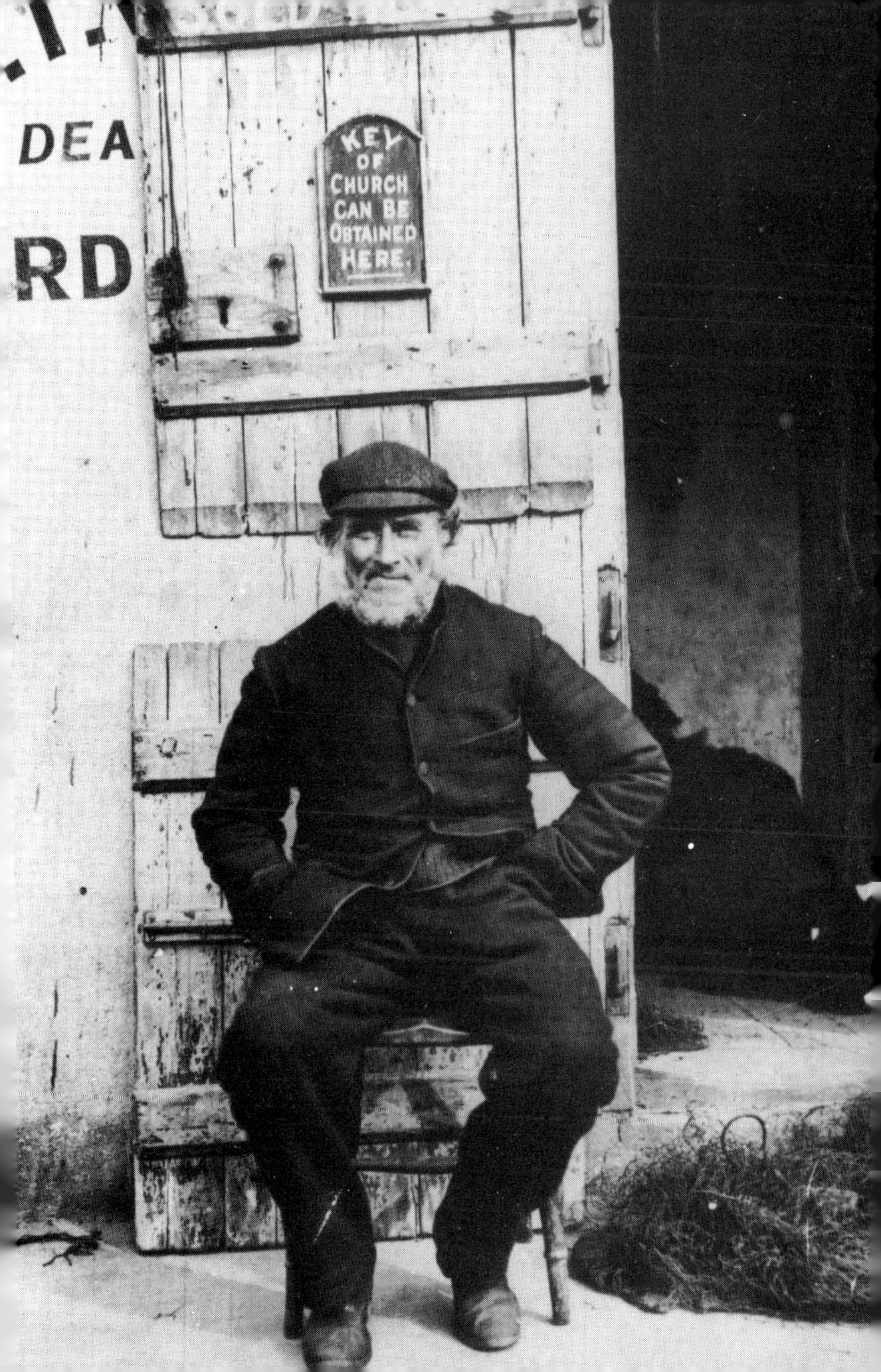
DEA
RD
KEY OF CHURCH CAN BE OBTAINED HERE.

From there we went back down to the Old Town, to Old Humphreys Avenue. I went to the Ebenezer Sunday School from there, in Tackleway, the next road up. There was a flight of steps led up past the Church and there was the girls' school. You could look through the window and see the girls sitting there. A ragged school I think it was.

Our next move was over to West Hill Cottages and from there I went to the Cavendish School. I must have been about five years old then. Before going there and going to the Waterloo School, when I was very small mother had taken me to the National School in All Saints Street, but apparently I kicked up such a row that she had to take me away. I would have been about two or three at the time. Another thing I remember about West Hill Cottages is having a bath in the washhouses there. We used to go up by the Hole-in-the-Wall pub. There was a row of cottages right behind Cobourg Place, and behind there in between the cottages, there was a rectangle with the washhouses at the top. Mother used to put the washing lines across the green there.

The funny thing is that I cannot remember moving at all, and yet I lived in at least nine different houses in my first seven years of life.

Next we went to Richardsons Cottages and after that to Providence Row where my brothers Robert John and Frederick Guildford were born. After that we went to Queens Road near Crew Davis which is where Supreme Stores is today, and I went to St Andrews School. I remember a fellow coming round selling fifty oranges for a shilling, but I don't recall whether we bought any!

Dad was a postman, when he could get a job. He was a very smart man. His buttons and boots and the peak of his cap, always shone when he went out, as if he was going on parade. Because he had been in the army he managed to get temporary jobs with the Post Office, but things were very precarious when he first came back from South Africa. He did anything he could. At one time he was working as a waiter at Feraris which used to be down the bottom of Havelock Road. I can remember standing outside with Mum and him bringing out different stuff, chips and things like that, to take home to eat.

Then he got the offer of a regular postal job if he would move to Battle, so we moved to Battle. Or rather to Telham first, to Primrose Cottage, just below the Church. That would have been about 1911 when I was eight years old. It was a slate cottage—it is still there—the usual thing like all the others I had lived in. A living room and a scullery downstairs and two small bedrooms upstairs, and the toilet was a hole up the garden as they used to be then. I had to walk all the way to Battle School in Marley Lane from there, although I was only eight years old. Mr Kemp was the headmaster in my days there.

Then we moved into Battle itself to 14 Lower Lake, and I was very pleased to be saved that long walk. My sister Ellen Frances was born at Lower Lake.

I remember the landlady at the Chequers Inn calling me over one day. She had a lot of jam that had gone sugary and she wondered if we would like it. Well Mum didn't turn her nose up at that, so we had a nice lot of jam. Things were not as tight as they had been since Dad got the regular postal job but there were six of us in the family then so anything extra was welcome.

I did rather like living at Battle because it was a different environment. I went out with the local lads birdnesting and that. I took some birds eggs home one time and cooked them. They were salty, not worth eating. Thrush and blackbird eggs. I managed to get out with the beaters one time, beating up pheasants. We got a bob for that—a bob was affluence! There were a lot of boys and men involved, and all the boys got a bottle of lemonade, a lump of bread and cheese and the bob. Men got more of course, but I was made up with my earnings.

At the bottom of Lower Lake was the gasworks managed by a Mr Christmas, and I used to go with some of the other lads watching them pull the coke from the furnaces. When they threw water on the coke the smell was awful.

Another thing I remember from our days at Battle was when Scott was at the Antarctic in 1912. Dad, being pretty patriotic, he cut out all the pictures from the Daily Mirror and framed them all and put them on the wall!

I went to the Methodist Sunday School at the bottom of Senlac Hill at Battle. I remember on one of our outings we went to Bexhill. It was a beautiful day and there were a lot of ships in the Channel. That was August 4th 1914, the outbreak of the First World War.

Dad would come over to Hastings sometimes on Sunday to get fish for breakfast, cycling and walking. He liked it cooked with bacon. It's very tasty done like that, I like it myself, fish and bacon. And if he got too many fish I would to go out and sell them. I never had any trouble doing that even though it was Sunday. Another thing I used to have to do was to go out and collect manure for his garden.

From Battle Dad used to take me to visit his sisters at Bulverhythe. They both lived in the old Coastguard Cottages. We walked up Tanyard Hill (we used to call the piece of road from the railway bridge to the top both names—Senlac Hill and Tanyard Hill) and didn't the tanyard stink! You could see the vats from the road lined up with piles of bark. On the right hand corner was a footpath and he knew the way down through Crowhurst and the seventeen arches. When we got there we always had to have Sunday dinner with Aunt Grace and Aunt Charity. The two sisters had married two brothers—the Johnson brothers—and they lived next door to each other in the Coastguard Cottages. They both went to Vancouver in 1912. They were my father's sisters and there was also Aunt Pet (christened Rachel, which she hated) and she married a Timms who I think was the brother of Cusher Timms who was a fisherman, a big man who lived just down past the Wellington pub in the High Street. There was a passage that led down into the Bourne. At the bottom there was the Diamond pub but in between were two or three cottages, and he lived in one of those. He was a big man and you always saw him with a bowler hat.

With the war starting in 1914 Dad was called up straight away, because he was in the reserve since the Boer War. He was sent to Dover as a recruiting sergeant. And of course Mum didn't want to stop in Battle. She didn't like it there and wanted to get back to the Old Town. Dad's sister had a place in the High Street—104c High Street— and as she was away working she let us come back there. We lived there at Aunt Pet's for a while but it was totally unsuited to us. It was only big enough for her, her husband (although she was a widow then) and her son. But Bobby Timms, her son had died young. So Aunt Pet had it on her own, although later Granny Gasson went to live with her.

I think that was the smallest place we ever lived in. It was up on the High Pavement up a little passage. There were four cottages—it was the end one—104, 104a, 104b, 104c. There was one room downstairs and no door into the kitchen (scullery) because there'd have been no room to open it. Stairs went out of the kitchen about two foot six inches wide up to two small bedrooms. You couldn't really call it a kitchen either. It was a kind of little lean-to thing, just big enough to have a sink under the window and a gas stove under the stairs. There was an attic which I suppose we may have used for sleeping, but you had to plod up a flight of steps outside and then about fifty to sixty yards to the toilet. At least it was our own, and did not have to be shared with any other families like some I have known. And it didn't have to be emptied either. They had the drains put in about 1897—I've got the receipt for that. Aunt Pet was living at 3 Kents Cottages at the time. I think she must have had it done before she got married to Robert Timms.

As soon as we got back to the Old Town we were down on the beach scrounging a few fish and things like that. And I remember Mum sending me to the bakery—Henry King and Feist up on Castle Hill—to get sixpennyworth of stale bread (usually just the bake from the day before). I didn't like having to do that but it was necessary. Money was short and Mum had now got four to feed beside herself. If I was unlucky I would have to go along to St Leonards, to bakers in North Street or Shepherds Street, to see if I could get some bread. That would last us for a while.

And then Mother got a place in Sinnock Square. It was at the bottom left of the steps, 2 Sinnock Square. That was where my other brother—John Stanley—was born. And I got a job helping the dairyman, Mr Edwards, just up the High Street. I must have been just about twelve then. It wasn't too bad. He used to have a truck and I helped him to push it up to the Paygate. That is where the Sussex Hotel is now at the top of Old London Road, just opposite the crossroads there. There used to be a tollgate there in days gone by. There would be three or four milk churns waiting there where the farmers had left them. We loaded them on the truck and pushed it back down the High Street. Mrs Edwards was a great sport. It was handy me living in Sinnock Square because I didn't wake up in the morning, so Mr Edwards would rap at the bedroom window with a pole and that would get me down. Mrs Edwards always had a cup of tea and a piece of toast waiting for me before I started. When we got back I took a little churn, about a gallon, and delivered to various places in the Old Town. I earned half a crown a week for that, and I gave it all to my mother. She might give me a copper or two back but she needed the money. Well Mum would have had an allowance from the army of course, and I suppose as Dad was a recruiting sergeant to begin with it might have been quite good, but he did like his pint of beer and when he kicked over the traces and was demoted to a private it would have been reduced.

He was in the Buffs and was in the trenches. He finished at Gallipoli. He was at Salonika. He saw quite a bit of service, but he wasn't

wounded. He had a lot of photos from the Boer War, but they mostly seemed to be rows of soldiers laid out waiting to be buried. Grandfather Gasson was a stonebreaker up on the Ridge, making for the roads and things like that. Dad left school at twelve to help his father and I suppose he got cheesed off with it, so he decided to join the army. While he was in the army he educated himself.

From Sinnock Square Mother moved down to 16 Bourne Walk, the last home of my childhood. We rented the house from Verrells who owned the rag and bottle and bone yard opposite. The smell from it made you wish it was further away! Next door to us were the Johnsons who had a kind of greengrocers in the Bourne between Upfields Yard and the Waterloo School, and on the other side was a war widow, Mrs Chapman, with her two children Lilian and Bert.

That was another small house—the front door was halfway up a passage which was about 20 feet long and opened into a yard where the communal washhouse was and also the one toilet for all the families— there were six of us then, the Johnsons had a big family of girls, and there were the three Chapmans.

When one opened the front door of the house one was facing a wall which was the back of the stairs. A door on the right led into the kitchen and another door on the left led into the front room. All the rooms had fireplaces and upstairs were two bedrooms—they were a little bigger. Us boys had the back bedroom—we had one bed for us three boys although later I had a single one on my own. Mother had a double bed in her room and a single one. We lay on straw palliasses with a flock mattress—that was more or less the custom in those days. Later on we had to use the front room as a bedroom when Nellie got bigger and the other girls came along. Otherwise we didn't really use that room—we lived in the kitchen. Mum had an old-fashioned cooker there—an old range with a tank at the side that boiled a couple of gallons of water and a copper and brass tap to empty it, and the oven was only about fifteen to eighteen inches. Just a very small range it was. Later on she had the gas put on—she had to pay for that of course—and she had a gas stove.

To get fuel for the old range I used to have to go to Stickells on a Saturday morning and hire a little push cart for a couple of coppers, and then go to the station and get two bobs' worth of coal. Stickells

Tom's grandfather, John Gasson

used to be at the top of Courthouse Street where it leads up into All Saints Street, more or less where the Wesleyan Church is today. I wasn't the only one—lots of boys used to do that. The washhouse was outside and there were three or four families to share it. Mum would take her turn on a Monday, or whatever. You had to take the water from the tap and carry it to the boiler to fill it up and, as I was the oldest one, I'd scrabble around to try to get it fired for her, with old paper, bits of wood, any old thing went in to try and get a boil. She'd be there nearly all day. There was only about twelve foot of yard and there was a big family of us and if it rained, oh dear, there was nothing to be done.

It was the same up at West Hill Cottages—the washhouses were at the back. You could go in there and have a wash but there was only cold water. You could take a kettle of hot water with you but that wouldn't get you far. I was only a kid then of course. It used to be the old hip bath in front of the fire up to the time we were ten or eleven. In later years I would go to the communal baths in the Bourne, pay fourpence, take a towel and a bar of soap. They did provide soap but we took our own anyway. Once a week that was that! And not many changes of clothing either. It just couldn't be done.

In the summer we didn't wear a lot anyway. We'd go to school in a pair of trousers and a shirt. Sometimes I was lucky if I had a pair of shoes. I have had to go to school more than once in my mother's shoes. I didn't like that much, because they were lace-ups.

I went to St Mary-in-the-Castle School now that we were settled in the Old Town. I was happy there and thought that we had very good teachers. The headmaster was Mr A.G. Taylor, there was a Mr Swingler. Mr Stevenson who was a councillor and owned the Sandringham Hotel just along from the Cinema de Luxe and my teacher, Mr Baldwin. He was an elderly man with a big class—certainly more than thirty—and if he caught you mucking about he would send you out to the headmaster who was the only one who caned you. It always struck me as funny afterwards. The headmaster had quite a large class, you'd open the door and sidle in and just stand there. You'd be in there about two minutes and the door would open and another boy would sidle in. In the end there might be a whole line of us. You had to listen to everything Mr Taylor said because when he was giving a lesson he wouldn't interrupt it until he was finished, and he'd be quite likely to ask you some questions on what he'd been talking about. But if you were all good little boys and listened and answered the questions, he'd say 'Go back to your classes' without giving you the cane. And then when I got back to my class Mr Baldwin would say 'Have you had the cane, Gasson?'. 'No, sir'. 'Well go back and get it'. And then you'd go back and Mr Taylor would say 'Didn't I send you back to your classroom a few minutes ago?'. I would say 'Yes, sir, but Mr Baldwin said I'd got to have the cane'. So Mr Taylor would say 'All right, come here' and he'd give you just a light one, a tap really. That was a good school. He didn't like caning us I don't think.

He did cane a boy once. I don't know what the boy had been up to but his mother came up the school and asked Mr Taylor to give him a thrashing. And he did it. It must have been something bad.

We used to go down to the Technical School in the Bourne once a week for two or three hours' tuition in carpentry. We would leave school about nine twenty, and sometimes we'd be a bit late, especially if there was snow about on the hills, or if we'd gone via the front which we were not supposed to do! I remember once trying to dodge the waves and getting soaked and have to race off home to get dry clothes. Luckily we lived quite near, so no one knew. On one occasion when there was snow about we were all late and Mr Dermott, the carpentry teacher (he wasn't a bad bloke—I met him later in life and had a long chat with him) said 'I'm not going to deal with you', so he marked us all late and sent us back with the register to Mr Taylor. Some bright spark had the notion of altering it but the trouble was it was indelible ink! The upshot of that was twenty two of us lined up—one on each hand! I didn't begrudge that. I wouldn't say we had more than we deserved. If I hadn't had the cane at least once a week I'd have thought my education was being neglected!

I suppose you could say we learnt the three Rs, reading, writing and arithmetic. There was no science, chemistry or physics. That came in much later. I don't think we even did algebra and we didn't measure things physically, it was all on paper. We didn't even have a playground to go out and measure. We used to go up on the West Hill for what was called organised games, but it didn't happen very often because there were so many of us. Our turn came around about once every three weeks. We used to do drill in the classroom. We had music and poetry and what was called silent reading. You took a book from the shelf and read it quietly on your own. I can remember lots of poems. 'I remember, I remember, the house where I was born' was one, and Gray's Elegy, but that was too long for kids to learn really. But other pieces like Casabianco I was more interested in. I enjoyed the music lessons but my trouble was that I had been to so many different schools that I had never got a proper education. St Mary-in-the-Castle did music but until I went there I had never done that. They were in the middle of a session and I couldn't get the hang of it. But I liked the singing. 'Sweet Lass of Richmond Hill', 'Men of Harlech', 'Early one morning'. We sang several Welsh songs I remember, I always liked those.

Every morning we started off with prayers—one hymn perhaps—just a little sermon—about a quarter of an hour that lasted. There were about forty in a class—you had to be good, but we were brought up like that. When you went into the class you got on with your lessons.

There were separate entrances for the girls and boys—you were not supposed to mix with the other sex when you were a child in those days! The sweetshop was dead opposite the boys' entrance; we were not supposed to go there, but of course we did on the rare occasions when we had a ha'penny to spend.

I don't think I ever played truant. I was happy enough at school. We might be a bit late getting down to the Technical School, or if we were sent out for misbehaving, we would hang about outside until the others came out and walk back to school with them. But I cannot remember ever playing truant deliberately. Well a man we used to call 'the school board' used to visit all the schools to check who was absent, and he'd call at your house. So if you did play truant you'd always be found out. If he saw children playing he would ask why they were not at school.

When I was at St Mary-in-the-Castle School, it must have been the first or second year of the war, they got us to collect a lot of horse chestnuts. They wanted to mash them down to get oil I believe. We didn't know what the end product was but they just wanted the boys to bring them in. Well, that was right up our street! All the schools did it I believe. But it was only the one year that we did it.

I was always with my pal Bill Sadler. He lived at 9 Croft Road—Arthur William Henry was his full name, but he was always called Bill. His mum and my mum were cousins. We always used to call his mum Aunt Fan and his dad Uncle Arthur. We used to spend ages of time together at the Fishmarket, on the beach, or climbing the cliffs. We used to wander over to Fairlight birdnesting, mushrooming or blackberry picking. We'd go along Rock-a-Nore and get a few dabs and cook them on a bit of old tin.

One evening, a group of us had been skylarking along there—there was Eddie Coleman, Donald Neal, me, Bill and one or two others—when someone suggested a last dip before we went home. No sooner said than done. We chucked our clothes down—well we only wore a pair of shorts and a shirt. I jumped in out of my depth and couldn't get back—just along the east harbour there. We used to spend quite a bit of time in the water but I couldn't swim more than a few strokes. I called that I would make for the breakwater—I thought I could climb on that but my friends thought I would be swept round. They shouted to me to float and they would fetch help. They were scared stiff in case I was swept away. I wasn't frightened myself—I just floated. Presently a soldier came in and tried to tow me ashore but he couldn't manage it. Somebody came with a boat—there was always somebody down there with a boat. Between the two harbours, the two walls, that was where the men and the boys could bathe. There used to be a notice up the west end telling ladies that nude bathing was in progress and not to go along there, more or less.

We boys never had a costume. We just chucked our clothes off and went in. There was a boat there in the daytime with a couple of chaps supplied by the Corporation. They used to hire out costumes to men if they wanted them. Anyway, I got into the boat. I wasn't too bad. I hadn't swallowed any water but I had floated a long way out the other side by the time they got to me. When I got to the beach it was full of people—there hadn't been a soul about before! I shoved my clothes on and rushed off home. And when I got there, there was mother just coming down. She had been up to the fish and chip shop in All Saint Street and someone had told her that I was nearly drowned. I don't know how long I was in the water but for mother to have got the news it must have been some time, because it was quite a distance from where we were. She had the baby—my brother Jack—in her arms and she was coming down to see what it was all about.

You can imagine how she must have felt when someone gave her that kind of news, because she had two brothers drowned at sea. One brother was Henry Adams drowned 1891. She was eleven years old at the time—she told me about it. They were all fishermen in her family. They came down the bottom of All Saints Street that night in 1891 when that storm was on but they couldn't do much, the men and the women. The other brother was drowned on the rocks at Fairlight—a boat had come ashore—I suppose they had gone to look at it. Well he never came home. They found his body. My mother had a photograph of it in the coffin. I didn't reckon much to that when I was a kid. There was also a cross frame with 'Henry Adams drowned at sea, 1891'. She always had that, but I don't know what happened to it.

One of the things we used to do was to go shrimping. We would hire a net from Jimmy Gallop at the bottom of All Saints Street. It cost a few coppers for a tide. It was a six foot one for boys but up to twelve foot for men. I would hope to get enough shrimps for the family to have a good meal, and enough to sell to pay for the hire of the net. You could always get winkles. We used to go right along the sewerage pipe towards Ecclesbourne to collect winkles off the rocks for Mum to boil for tea. I didn't really care too much about them. Too fiddly to get out.

All my uncles were fishermen so I could always reckon to get some herrings by giving them a hand. Harts had what we called a 'Deeze' to smoke them on and turn them into bloaters. You'd get a stick from him and thread twenty to twenty-four herrings on to it and leave them with him for a day or two. He only charged a few coppers. If we got too many dabs we would clean them and hang them outside the bedroom windows to dry out. They were all right barring the flies. And they didn't taste as good as the fresh ones of course. They were a bit dry. Coussens had a 'Deeze' as well. The fish shop was in All Saints Street and sometimes Dad would say 'Nip down Coussens and see if they have got any 'tietails''. Well they were bloaters but a bit deformed. In other words if when they were taken off the sticks the heads were broken a bit, they were tied by the tails in bundles and sold cheaper. Of course when we left Sinnock Square I left Mr Edwards milk job, so I had more time to go on the beach.

I remember one day when they must have had some terrific catches because the beach was filled up with herrings and the fish ladies counting them into barrels. Anyone who has anything to do with fishing earns their money. We used to go down sometimes after the punts had gone out for sprats to help pull them back up on the beach and sometimes they would come back with nothing. Sometimes in 1916 or 1917 two steam trawlers came here and also some bigger sailing boats than ours. They anchored off the west side of the harbour arm and their fish was brought ashore in boxes by the ferryboats. Most of

Tom's three uncles—the Adams' brothers (standing from right)

HASTINGS FISHERMEN

that was emptied in lumps down the beach—there wasn't as much beach as there is now—and auctioned by Jack Adams.

He was a big man—he wasn't the only auctioneer—I can't remember the name of the other man, but he wore glasses. I was fascinated by the auctioneer. He would always start off at a price that he knew no one would buy at and gradually come down to what he considered a reasonable price and then slow down. I've known him to come to what he considers rockbottom, and then buy it himself. Of course when the Lightfoot Refridgeration Company came to Rock-a-Nore Road that was a help to the fishermen.

A lot of fish was cleaned in the market at that time. There was a large corrugated shed with a kind of tip-up truck for the fish guts to be put in and that used to be taken to the end of Rock-a-Nore road and tipped in the sea. At that time it was the practice for anything to be dumped there. Before the cart was taken away we used to take out the huss that had been skinned to take out the flaps, as we called them because when the huss was skinned a nice piece was left—about six inches by three inches or six inches by two inches—they left it because it was a bit of a job to skin. If you could get some they were quite tasty. Another thing—but you had to buy them—was squinches. They looked like small scallops, and perhaps they were, and when you had boiled them they looked like a poached egg and very tasty they were. But it was seldom we got any of those! Grandfather Adams said they came from the Diamond Ground.

I used to like to watch the horses pulling up the boats. They were lovely animals stabled at Rock-a-Nore. The boats wouldn't be drawn up unless the fishermen were going ashore for a few days. If they were going off again shortly the boats would be anchored 'in the roads'. That was Grandfather's expression, but it meant that they were anchored in the harbour. When they were going out again, the men would get two or three barrels of water from the East Well under the lift. I remember that some of the fishermen had huge leather boots that came right up to their thighs, with a lappet on to help pull them on. Sometimes the fishermen would have a sports meeting at the bottom of High Street along towards Rock-a-Nore. There would be races and things like climbing the greasy pole. I can remember two chaps racing each other up greased poles set about eight feet apart—they each had a bit of rope to help.

Bonfire night was really something in those days. I think Ore and

Bohemia had their own guys. I know the Old Town did, and there was quite a procession along the front and of course the glorious burn up on the beach with fireworks flying everywhere. They never burnt the head of the guy though, I suppose they had spent too much time making it.

We didn't have much in the way of toys when I was a child but I cannot remember that I was ever bored. Bill Sadler and myself, we used to wander all over what is now the country park or go down on the beach to help the fishermen or collect shrimps. During the school holidays we would go to the station and ask holiday-makers if we could carry their bags for them—I used to ask the ladies because usually their bags were lighter! People who were strangers would ask us where a certain road was and we would take them to the Memorial and tell them which tram they needed. We usually made a bob or two like that.

Outside the Waterloo School, and opposite Rogers the sweetshop, was a fair sized bit of ground where mostly the girls and smaller children played. Boys played tipcat in the gutter or in the ring, also buttons in a ring. You would have a piece of slate on the pavement to slide them out with. I had a hoop made of iron, girls mostly had them made of wood. They were about two foot in diameter but sometimes the girls had bigger ones. You ran up and down with a skid to bowl them along. Tipcat was a piece of wood which you hit with a bat. Not really a good idea in the crowded Old Town, but we used to have it. And we used to go over the reservoir back of Ecclesbourne Glen with a toy boat to sail on the water. And we used to try to catch fish—roach I think they were—with a worm tied to a piece of string—I can't remember ever catching one!

We used to go to the pictures if we could afford it. Later when I started work I went a bit more—saw Mary Pickford in Daddy Longlegs, Charlie Chaplin in Shoulder Arms, Tom Mix and W.S. Hart in the first westerns. We used to get a three hour programme then with a big film, Pathe Pictorial, Mutt and Jeff, Keystone Cops and Max Sennett's bathing beauties. We had some good laughs especially when the film broke down and the pianist in the pit had to go on playing until it was mended. Bill Freeman, who had to keep order in the gods since some of the lads were not above slinging orange peel and other stuff on the wealthier patrons below, was a big man and if he spotted anyone misbehaving they were out. You didn't argue with him. He was a fishmonger by trade and in later life had a shop in Bohemia.

In Queens Road near the cricket ground, where the bus station is now, there used to be a fair sometimes, and in the summer a concert party took over. Wallis Arthurs they were called. There would be a big marquee with a stage at one end and rows of seats. The first part of the show was always in pierrot dress. We used to go occasionally, but after a couple of times you knew the programme. But it was nice for visitors. The pier bandstand was a very popular rendezvous for young people on summer evenings—the military bands were very popular. Also at that time—about 1919—the Salvation Army used to march from St Andrews Square to Caroline Place for an open air service on Sunday evenings. They always had a large audience. And for a diversion there were always one or two cranks on the beach, waving banners spouting 'The end of the world is nigh'. They may have been serious but the spectators were not, so you had to admire their pluck.

Also at that time, just after I had left school, Bill and I used to go to concerts in the Market Hall in George Street, over the market area that has just been renovated. Theatrical companies would sometimes hire it. And at the Cinema de Luxe there used to be—I think it was called—the Hastings and St Leonards Municipal Orchestra, under various conductors—two I remember were Basil Cameron and Julius Harrison. Before the White Rock was built they played at the cinema De Luxe as at that time the pictures were not allowed to be shown on Sundays. Actually the White Rock Pavilion was built with this orchestra in mind. They used to play semi-classical stuff with some classical light kind of things, because they didn't want symphonies in the Old Town! Things like the William Tell overture, Ballet Egyptian, and of course Gilbert and Sullivan. Tuneful and not too heavy. Fred Verrell was one of the people who used to sing there—he was the son of the rag and bone people we rented our house from.

A year or two on I can remember a cloud of smoke drifting across the town one Sunday, and when we got to the beach Hastings Pier was well alight. We could see people shoving stuff off. We found out afterwards that some of the troops stationed in the town helped the firemen to put out the flames.

Miss Burford and Miss Breed in the High Street were two old ladies who came from families connected with the brewery industry. Breed's Brewery was in the Bourne. They would always give us a Bible class on a Sunday afternoon, and tea and cakes afterwards. And sometimes we would go to the Band of Hope in the Croft for a magic lantern show—

we knew all the places where we could get something for nothing, the way most kids do.

We used to have Quaker Oats for breakfast and bread and butter; sometimes an egg. Bread and butter for tea. Possibly with shrimps or winkles if I had been able to get any. Dinners, well we had alot of stews when Dad was home. He liked stews and curries. You could never get a curry hot enough for him. If he had a stew he would still plonk his curry on top of it. More like a peppery stew than the pukka curry you might have today. On Sundays we nearly always had a roast. When we lived down the Bourne I can remember taking the roast, piece of beef or whatever you had, with the potatoes round it, up to a bakers for them to cook. Brookers or Banksons—they were just up the top of the passage in the High Street. You took it up before ten and then dashed up with a cloth later and collected it. And Mum would put on a great big duff—plain suet duff—and you'd eat that with the meat to fill you up. Any that was left was fried the next day and eaten with jam.

There was a milkman living at the top of All Saints Street and he would come round with his yoke across his shoulders and two buckets, selling skimmed milk. I don't remember how much it was, a penny or tuppence a pint—and Mum would buy some of that. That would just about go in the oven in a big dish—a rice pudding mostly there. Sometimes tapioca. The roast dish of course, it just wouldn't go in the oven to feed all of us, that's why I had to take it up to the baker. Dad always used to cook the vegetables! He used to clean them outside in the bath. I used to have to go up to Granny Gasson at Ore and get some vegetables and rhubarb and gooseberries. She had a lot of stuff up there. Sometimes on Sunday I would have to go down to Buttons and get watercress for tea. Dad was very fond of that. Other than that the fare was pretty plain. In the weekdays, apart from the stews Mother might make a meat pudding or a pie.

During the First World War with Dad away, and having such a big family on a low income, Mum did find it difficult to feed us all. I used to go down to the soup kitchen. That was down the Creek Steps underneath the Fishermen's Club. I would take the big jug that we had in the handbasin to wash in, and get that filled up with soup for the family for twopence or threepence. If they didn't have any there I would go up to Croft Road where there was another soup kitchen under the Church Hall there. Most people did this when they were hard up. Sometimes I've gone down with a halfpenny and had a bowl of soup. Taken a bit of bread with me. And that would be my dinner.

We always seemed to be queuing up in the First World War. I remember that we had a tin of bloater paste for Sunday breakfast. That cost a penny or tuppence. If you had any Quaker Oats there wasn't enough sugar to go on it to make it sweet. No jam. Just the blackberry and apple. No sugar to make a real jam. It was just like stewed stuff. I think that may have been a combination of lack of money and shortage of things in the shops.

When I look back on childhood I remember it as a very happy time. There was never money for much—birthdays, perhaps we might get a bar of chocolate, or a penny to spend. We never had a cake. At Christmas we hung up a stocking, we'd get an orange, two or three nuts, perhaps a whistle or a pencil and a piece of paper. Never anything that cost more than twopence or threepence. Christmas cards were unheard of then, although I have a few birthday cards that I've kept over the years. We never had a lot but we were never really hungry. The food was plain most of the time but we were never starving.

At Christmas when Grandfather Gasson slaughtered his pigs we always had a nice piece of pork. Granny Gasson used to make a delicacy called 'Fleed cakes' that were a great favourite with everyone except me—I could never understand why everyone enjoyed them— they were like a kind of suet pudding thing—not sweet enough.

There were many shops then. Just down the steps from Sinnock Square to the right was the High Street Post Office and to the left Ockendens the butcher, with Mitchells the fish and chip shop, just beyond. It was always busy in those days—1915—because of all the Canadian soldiers in the town. Where Edwards dairy was is now the Post Office. Mr Edwards also had a sweet shop where the cake shop is now down by Post Office Passage. I remember that he had a large cylinder behind the counter with gas in it that he used for making various mineral waters—he had lots of flavours. He called them 'Monsters' I remember. These were much larger than the bottles with the glass marble that you had to push in. I think he charged tuppence for these monsters. It was his wife's sister used to run the shop for him. There was a pork butcher too that sold delicious pasties for tuppence each. Up a litle way, where Mitchell's shop is was quite a large drapers shop run by Charlie Eaton. George Street was a very busy shopping centre in those days. There were lots of barrow boys selling rabbits for about a shilling, and fish and vegetables. I remember a man standing outside a shop selling eggs from a huge box. And other shops had them too. And inside was butter and margarine—we usually had to make do with Mayco margarine—and biscuits in boxes about a foot square. Huntley and Palmer, and McVitie and Price. And broken biscuits. I used to like sampling all the different kinds! Hickman's the butcher was just across the road—they had a whopping big chopping block in the centre about five feet in diameter and carcases of lambs, pigs and beef hanging all round. And me going for a shillingsworth of meat for a pie and hoping to get enough for a pudding too! Sometimes I would ask for a sheep's pluck—that is liver, heart and lungs which were boiled, or I would go to the pork butcher for some pork rinds for soup. Next to the Anchor pub on the other side of the passage was the British and Argentine Meat Company, and on Saturday night they used to auction off any left over meat. The butcher would hold up a lump of beef or mutton or whatever and say something like 'Well give me five bob for that', and if there were no takers he would add a bit and say 'Well now five bob!'. There was always a crowd round the shop.

And the shops stayed open very late then. And just past the passageway and into West Street was a fish and chip shop which was there for a good many years. There were two pawn shops in George Street, one each side of the road, Stratfords and Wrights. Many a woman would take something in on a Saturday night—watch, ring, medals, any gold item—to buy something for Sunday dinner, and then hope to redeem it next week. You went in a side door and there was a long passageway with three or four cubicles. 'Could you advance me thirty shillings on this?'. He'd say 'No. Give you fifteen shillings'. In the winter time Joe Mamonne and Harry Valente set up their braziers in George Street selling hot roast chestnuts and baked potatoes. In the summer they would switch to icecream and hokey pokey. That is a kind of ice cream in a cone—you don't see it today but it must have lasted well past my childhood because my daughters used to sing 'Hokey pokey penny a lump. Enough to make a donkey jump'.

When we moved to Bourne Walk I became familiar with more shops. Just beyond the Diamond pub was a little sweet shop—well more like a front room really with a large shelf inside. And before purchasing much consideration had to be given to the choice of sweets. Bullseyes, gobstoppers in various colours, liquorice, sherbet dabs, scorched peas, and there were always marbles or pea shooters. A penny never went far enough. That shop was typical of many in the Old

Town—there seemed to be one at the top of every passage, and there were a lot of passages! Well old lady Rea lived right opposite the passage in Bourne Walk and we used to buy ice cream from her. She always called out 'Hallo Tommy' to me. Her husband and first two sons were ice cream merchants. They were not related to the Di Marcos but in the same clan. Further down the Bourne was Mr Pankhurst the grocer, and when you bought goods from him he gave you a green card with various prices on it. He used clippers to punch out the value of the goods bought and when all were punched out you were allowed so much in free groceries. I reckon Green Shield pinched his idea. Then of course there was Mrs Button with her watercress. She would sit on a chair inside her front door with a huge basket of watercress. I was sent down many a time to get two pennyworth for tea. Further down the Bourne one came to the police station with Sergeant Roberts in charge and also the fire station at the bottom of Courthouse Street. Breeds Brewery was in the Bourne too.

In All Saints Street there was a general store run by 'Fat Man Kent' as we called him, and in there you could get a pennyworth of anything. Corned beef, pickles, jams, all sold loose, paraffin, matches, tobacco. Of course he really served a purpose because if you were very hard up you could buy very small amounts in there. But the smell of that shop with all those items jumbled up fairly took your breath away. Rubies, the place where Grandfather Gasson took the pigs for curing, was at the top of a passage into All Saints Street. Latterly the Rea Brothers took over. Also in All Saints Street there was a man who mended broken china with a rivet. People couldn't afford to throw things away then. Jimmy Gallops where we hired the shrimp nets was at the bottom of All Saints Street.

Down the bottom by Crown Lane, was Glazier, the Punch and Judy man. He used to set up his booth on the beach near Claremont and Mrs Glazier would take up the collection. The rowing club was along there too, under the Parade, before they built the car park.

There used to be hawkers lined up all along Queens Road on the shops' side selling fish, vegetables and flowers. I think the shop people complained about them because they had to go to the other side and then around into South Terrace and finally, like old soldiers, they faded away. One of the last to go was Teddy Salmon who managed to hang on at the corner of Marks and Spencers. They were all locals, Dickie Gowan, Baldy Rich, the two Lees. Their family was here until a few years back—umpteen of them there were, the Lees. Also, just above Watson's, was a penny bazaar, quite a large shop, although some of the items were tuppence or threepence. I suppose as things got dearer they were unable to keep to these prices and had to close down. I think Mosleys in Castle Street must be one of the oldest shops there. I can remember it from my childhood—it had a whopping great saw, about eight feet long, as a sign. Opposite them was a grocer called Revells and they had a gramophone and you could hear that gramophone right along Wellington Place.

There used to be an old chap went along Rock-a-Nore with a little cart to the end of the groyne, until he found some soft clay which he made into lumps about four by two by two, like a small brick. Then he went all over the place selling pipe clay, penny a lump. This wasn't for making pipes; at that time women used this clay to smarten up their hearths and doorsteps. I suppose that just about saved him from the workhouse.

There were no lights in the house in Bourne Walk—we had to use oil lamps. A fellow came round pushing a large tank on a barrow selling oil. Others came selling muffins or crumpets from a basket and in the summer there was always someone selling shrimps or whelks. Steve Brown used to come down from Ore with his barrow 'Any scissors, knives to grind?'. And of course the rag and bone man came round with a barrow and a bell. He would take anything at all—jars, bones, rags, rabbit skins, bottles. He would have handmade small windmills to give to the kids in exchange for a jam jar. And he would use a steelyard to weigh the rags—halfpenny a pound. Blizzards in Winding Street or West Street used to process the bones—there was a terrible smell from there at times.

Most of the street lamps round the Bourne area were lit by gas and every evening and morning the gaslighter put them on and off. He had a pole about eight foot long. On the front though, they were electric. The lights seemed to be in a glass bowl. The workman had a thing that looked like a starting handle, you could lower the lamp from its fitting and then put in what looked like a carbon pencil, and wind the lamp up again.

If you were ill, unless it was really bad, you didn't have the doctor. Shippams the Chemist in the Old Town stood in for a doctor more or less. Mum would send you up 'Ask him for something for so and so' and he would make up a mixture. For colds or upset tummies, that kind of thing. Every Friday night, after we had had our baths, before we went to bed, Mum would give us all a dose of something liquorice powdery, horrible it was. That was general, everybody did it. Dose of something every week, whether you wanted it or not. And for colds there would be something on the old stove, like onions, vinegar and brown sugar. It was terrible.

I cannot remember any of my brothers being born. I must have been very naive because I can remember taking money up to the Laurels, and I didn't realise what it was for for many years after. The midwives had to be paid in advance or they didn't come. And that hadn't changed when my own children were born. And when you went to summon them to the birth, like as not you had to carry the black bag for them too!

I used to belong to the St Clements Church Lads' Brigade. We were affiliated to the King's Royal Rifles. There were sessions once or twice a week. Our officer was Captain Harmon, and he was under Major Maggs over at Blacklands Church—their headquarters were at Hughenden Road. We used to drill with them and go on manoeuvres— we were made up with that! Proper drill, we were more or less army

Lads' Brigade

cadets although we didn't realise it then. I've looked at the photographs and we were just kids, about thirteen or fourteen. One or two were older lads like Judge from the bakers shops in the High Street, and Bill Reeves.

One of the highlights of my life as a boy was going on a Church Parade to Winchester, of all places. I had never been anywhere so nice. There were lots of Church Lads' Brigades affiliated to the King's Royal Rifles, and we all marched round Winchester and then went into the Cathedral The Regimental Band was playing, and the organ. One just marvelled at it. They played the Trumpet Voluntary, and Handel's March in Scipio, although I didn't know the names then. We had guns, Lee Enfields from the Boer War. There were racks of them. This was no mucking about, this was the genuine thing. There was an enormous number of people being killed in that war and I suppose they were bringing us on like ... lucky it ended. I was too young for that war and more or less too old for the next one.

In 1916 and 1917 I spent most of my spare money on boys' books. Mostly the Magnet and the Gem were popular, and when they were read I would go up to Cheshire's in Queens Road to swap them for some I had not seen. They always had a lot of boys' books. I read a lot at that time and my mother used to like to look at them as well. The old Comic Cuts, Weary Willy and Tired Tim were always good for a laugh.

Walking up High Street on the right hand side one came to the stables where the horses were being groomed and also the carriages and wagonettes being cleaned. Then there was a piece of ground up behind the Wilderness at the top of High Street where it picked up with All Saints Street, with the horse trough. There was an iron cup on a chain where you could have a drink. There was a spout shaped like a lion's head—the spout came from the lion's mouth. The market cross was in the middle of the road.

The last house on the left adjoining Torfield was used by Arthur Dicker (Bill Sadler's uncle) as a coal yard. He had a stable there for his horse and cart. Other horses were there. I believe the doctors kept their stable along the back of the yard. At that time, with the elms down to the bottom of Old London Road, it looked very attractive. Just past Torfield, going up one came to Bates' Field—that's what we called it—and mostly at that time cows used to be grazing there. Coming back down on the left was the pound or compound where stray animals were taken to be claimed, and mostly there seemed to be some in there. Also along there blind Henry Hudson had a spot where he played the gramophone. There were quite a few who played an instrument. One poor devil had a peg leg and a music box strapped to his back. He wore several medals.

Mr Taylor was responsible for getting me my first job. At that time one had to pay a premium—anything from twenty pounds to twenty-five pounds for an apprenticeship, so that was out. He suggested I go down to Watsons, the jewellers in Queens Road because he knew they wanted a boy, and he wrote me a good reference which I still have. I went for an interview and got the job and I stayed there for four or five years. It was quite good there. Mr Watson had to do a bit of war work, and there were two women there, Miss Chivers and Mrs Ashingdon. When there was nothing to do they would let me go and watch cricket in the Priory Meadow. This would be about 1919. When the war ended there was real cricket there and I suppose that I saw some of the top names over there. There had been another chap there when I first went, watchmaking, and if he hadn't got called up after a few months I would have learned to do that too.

KATHLEEN SHOESMITH

Born 1904

I was born at 30 North Street, St Leonards, next door to the British Queen. It is still there. It was a six roomed house with a passage. There were two rooms and kitchen downstairs and three bedrooms upstairs. There was a backyard downstairs and my father had an allotment, although we always referred to it as a garden, at the top of Albany Road. They were more like a garden in those days divided from each other with little hedges, not the open affairs you see today. We lost that when they built Boscobel Road North on the site. We had a lodger, Miss Shipman, an invalid lady who had the front ground floor room. My mother used to look after her. My parents paid ten shillings weekly for rent, and five shillings taxes.

I can remember living next door to the British Queen and running in there to ask for a biscuit for my little sister. The woman who served in there seemed old to me then, but I suppose she was probably only in her teens.

My father was born in 1875 in Shepherd Street. He was a paperhanger and decorator and so was his brother George, and their father before them. In those days you stuck to one trade, it wasn't a mixture as it is now. George had his 'sheepskins'. That was what they called the articles you had as an apprentice. I think I may still have them somewhere because they came down to my brother and I have a lot of his things. George was my father's older brother, and he worked for Cruttendens before it was Eldridge and Cruttendens, or maybe it was Eldridge before. He went up to London before the First World War and settled in Chiswick. I remember when Grandmother left in 1922 to go to Reading, some wallpaper turned up that George had sent home. It had been used for papering the royal stables at Buckingham Palace! I suppose it would be for rooms over. Beautiful bright blue paper with gold crowns on it. My grandmother had kept it for years, because she was seventy-two when she left Hastings, but we used it to line our drawers. Grandfather died in 1911. He was James Perigo

Pilbeam, and he came down from Sandhurst with his father who was a widower and his sister. Great grandfather was a blacksmith and he set up his forge and helped to build the Palace Pier. He made the ironwork for it. Of course it is gone now. And as for my father, he had more work that he could cope with in the summer and nothing in the winter. As a child I can remember him often having big houses to do and, especially in the summer time, we used to take his tea to him so he could work all the hours of daylight; and sometimes later, he was a rare one for candles. Us girls used to love taking Dad's tea up to him—we would run all over those lovely empty houses—those big houses in Pevensey Road and Albany Road I'm talking about. When it was cold he'd have a row of just ordinary candle stubs along the mantelpiece—he used to say there was a lot of heat in candlepower.

When I was nearly three years old the family moved round to 11 Kenilworth Road. I don't remember the move because I was sent away to stay with my grandparents at Willisborough—I had a sister a year and seven months younger than myself then, and I suppose it was easier for my parents just to have the baby. I had my third birthday at Willisborough. I can remember being frightened by the pig—well at three years old you aren't very big are you? I remember seeing the pig being taken off to be killed. After that I wouldn't go out of the house even though I knew there was no pig in the sty. My grandparents had been farmers and they always kept one pig in a sty down the garden.

My parents might have stayed in North Street, but on one occasion when my father's mother was staying with us we walked along Kenilworth Road to the 'garden' in Albany Road, and these houses were up to let at thirty-five pounds per year, plus taxes of seven pounds which made forty-two pounds in all. They were very nice houses then, with ten rooms on four floors, and a little garden. Grandmother said to Mother 'You are paying fifteen shillings a week now. You could have twice the number of rooms for a shilling or two extra a week'.

And that is how we came to move to Kenilworth Road. My father always said it took two years' rent to do it up. Lovely big rooms it had and it was completely decorated when we moved in. On the top floor there were three rooms and a big landing, then three or four steps down to the half landing where there was a little three-cornered sink for water. It used to freeze up in the winter because it was on the east side. Then you came down to the next floor that we called the drawing room floor—there were two large rooms there. The next floor down was the hall floor where you came in at the front door, there were three rooms there, and then there was the basement, which was not really a basement, it was lovely down there. The only toilet was on the hall floor and there was a draw off tap in there. We had an outside toilet downstairs.

When my parents first took the house they went in with another family, the Merrifields. We had the basement and the top floor and also the hall floor front room for Miss Shipman. Mrs Merrifield had the room beyond Miss Shipman for her kitchen and the little room at the top of the stairs to the basement, which we always called the back office, was used by Mr Merrifield's old blind mother as a bedroom. And they had the two big rooms on the drawing room floor as bedrooms. It was a stupid way to arrange things, but I suppose young Mrs Merrifield wanted the use of the toilet on the hall floor because they had three small children.

Later my father's parents took number nine, and Grandmother used to do a lot of letting. She had some very good visitors. Grandfather died in 1911 but Grandmother stayed there on her own until 1922, when she went to Reading to keep house for her youngest son who had never married. They didn't own their house—only rented it. I don't know what rent they paid. I don't think I ever heard it mentioned. I always thought it was not quite as nice as our house. The road was wider where we were. Our garden was bigger too—it was the biggest back garden. We had grass and grew raspberries—white raspberries they were called although really they were more of a honey colour. Beautiful flavour they had. And we had Madonna lilies and chrysanthemums. After father died Maisie took it over. I can remember the tomatoes she grew there during the war.

My parents brought Miss Shipman with them to Kenilworth Road. They wheeled her round in a bathchair. This was in 1907 and she died in 1917. She had the nice big room inside the front door and she never left it again. They used to get her off the bed and into a chair, but she never dressed. She used to wear a little nightcap all the time and all her things went to the laundry so she must have had some money. My mother used to look after her until my brother and youngest sister were born after the First World War and then my father would not let her get up. Miss Shipman used to pay an old lady one shilling a night to sit with her then. I was still at school then but they knew me at the Post Office in Kings Road and I used to collect Miss Shipman's pension for her. Five shillings a week she had. She had some nice bits of furniture and when she died her relatives—people called Brimley from Frimley in Surrey who visited her occasionally—gave these to mother.

My mother had to work hard and when my father died she had no pension, just the house to live on. She cooked for her boarders as well—that is more the summer visitors. The permanent boarders mostly did their own cooking. Mother did not like full boarding the holiday people at all really. Most people charged thirty-five shillings weekly but mother insisted on two guineas for full board. She didn't mind cooking their food if they bought it themselves, but she always felt as if she wasn't giving them sufficient. Londoners always seemed to eat so much meat and so much of everything. Well they were on holiday I suppose.

It doesn't bear thinking about now, but on the top floor we had a blind lady, Miss Harvey. I remember she kept her coal in a tea chest. They all had little oil stoves for cooking and some of them had coal fires. There were fireplaces in every room. It is a wonder the house never caught fire. Miss Harvey had a sister who worked and when she retired they took a couple of rooms lower down the road at number six and kept house together. Miss Harvey could read braille but when you think of her managing on her own four floors up!

All that winter, 1910/11, we had the Miss Maggs with us. They had the top three rooms and the big drawing room. They were gentry folks really I suppose. One of them was a missionary, home on a year's furlough from Durban. Their brother was the rector or curate at St Paul's Church which used to be in Ellenslea Road. It has been pulled down now, and Norfolk House is there. St Paul's wasn't big enough for all the people who wanted to go—which would have included all the maids from the big houses, so they built St Peter's up at the top to take the overflow. My mother-in-law would have gone there when she was in service with Mrs Pritchard at 38 Church Road.

In 1911 Nurse Neill came in with us, and she had the two top rooms of all, both the front rooms, a smallish one and a large one and the landing, and blind Miss Harvey had the back one on that floor. My sister Maisie and I had the back office as our bedroom. Mum had the room that had been the Merrifield's kitchen as her bedroom and old Miss Shipman was in the front. Maisie and I were in that room for a long time and then in the twenties after Miss Harvey had left, we had the top back bedroom for a time. In 1913 a friend who my mother had met whilst in service, Miss Whiting, always called Aunt Emily, took one of the rooms on the third floor. Aunt Emily had kept house for her father who had a pub in Green Street Green in Kent, and after he died she came to us. The room had been furnished for holiday letting and Aunt Emily had all her furniture in there too and you couldn't move, but as she took positions away most of the time—this was during the First war and she went as cook to families—it did not matter too much. And when we were very busy with holiday-makers we were allowed to make use of the room and sleep there so our rooms were free. And we had Mrs Reeves in the room that had been Miss Shipman's. She had lovely geraniums all round in window boxes.

The houses came on the market in 1913 and my parents bought theirs, so they owned it until 1947 when my mother died. My father died in 1935 two months after King George V died.

I had two sisters and one brother all younger than myself. Maisie was born in April 1906, so she wasn't two when we moved to Kenilworth Road. My brother was born April 1913—the night Levetleigh was burned down—and Joyce was born June 3rd 1915. She was like a little doll when she was small and I used to love to dress her and take her out. She was such a docile little thing until she was four and a half when she caught diptheria and was in the Sanatorium for four weeks and four days over Christmas. There was a bad epidemic of it here December 1919. When she came out the iron seemed to have entered her soul. We don't know what happened to her in there, but we wondered if they were tied to their beds. If my mother corrected her while we were sitting at the table she would get down and put her face in the corner. But she is the one who has done things. She has travelled widely.

My brother was Arthur James Ambrose Pilbeam. I remember at his Christening, I was about eight at the time, when the vicar said 'Name this child' my mother said Arthur James and my father piped in 'Ambrose'. Arthur was my father's name—he had only the one, James was his father's name and Ambrose was his brother, although he was Alfred Ambrose. So my brother got landed with AJAP. My sister Maisie—who was a year and seven months younger than me—and myself were kept very much alone. We were never allowed to play in the street. Our younger brother and sister, who were children after the First World War, had an entirely different upbringing. When I first went to school when I was five apparently I was a little horror. I didn't want to go and I screamed. It wasn't very far, the Mercatoria School where my father had gone before me, and his brothers and sisters. So they let my sister start with me although she was only three years and five months old, for the company of someone I knew. And she liked it and stayed.

I carried on there until I was fourteen. In those days you stayed at the same school. There was the infants with about four classes. When you were six or seven you went upstairs into the Elementary School, I think that's what it was called. There was Standard 1 with a little room on their own; Standards 2 and 3 in another room; then 4 and 5, and after that you went into the Headmistress' room which was Standards 6, 7 and X7. I remember that I had the cane once when I was in Standard 4. I never went in Standard 5, I skipped from 4 and was sent up to 6. I think I was fairly bright. We had a teacher in Standard 4, Miss Martin, I can't remember what I had done, but she lost her temper and sent me to the Headmistress, Miss Warren, for the cane. Miss Warren was one of the old school. She left that year. I went home to my mother and said 'I can't go back to school this afternoon. I can't ever go back. I've had the cane!'. I was so horrified. But my mother said 'Of course you are going back' and I jolly well had to go!

When Miss Warren left we had another headmistress, Miss Clara or Clarice Miles. She had letters after her name, some of which she said were a very rare thing. LLRCP was one, and Lady of Licensed Arts. I don't know how old she was but she was a clever person and dedicated. She taught us for four years. She would start to give us a lecture. And afterwards she would say 'Well that wasn't quite what I had intended to have done but perhaps it will do you more good'. She taught us a little bit of French after school—she wanted to make a little extra money I suppose. It cost sixpence but that was quite enough in those days. That would have been about 1916 or 1917. I won a prize for writing an essay on nature—the second prize I think it was—a copy of Robinson Crusoe. I've still got it! I had to go along to the Brassey Institute to collect it. That was quite an event! There weren't many scholarships in those days but I did swot up for it, did homework. I think you had to be thirteen to go in for it. We had an Honours Board but there were not many names on it in those days. Unfortunately on the day I should have taken the examination I was not at school. Maisie and I both had it. Our hands peeled. It may have been scarlet fever, but my mother maintained, and she had had scarlet fever as an adult so she wasn't silly about it, that it was the sulphur tablets we were taking as a spring medicine that caused it. We did go out wearing gloves, because we used to take the younger ones along the sea front, but I remember that we peeled all over. I think we may have been run down because the food was not very good then. Decent food was not plentiful. I can remember queuing up in the snow at the Maypole for margarine in January 1917 with the town full of Canadian soldiers.

I was at school when the Armistice was signed. I remember the Headmistress saying it was signed the eleventh hour of the eleventh day of the eleventh month, 1918.

I don't ever remember being hungry when I was a child. I think we probably ate better than a lot of people. We used to have a rabbit once a week. I don't remember fish and chips from a fish shop but I know my father used to bring in fish and my mother must have cooked it, but I don't remember it being fried much. We used to have shrimps for Sunday tea. My father used to order them and a man would bring them live. Uncooked they look terrible—little grey things. Mother used to rinse them in the sink and put them in a great big pot of water on the kitchener. She would stir them with a red hot poker. They don't take long and they are lovely—your own home cooked ones.

We always had puddings. Suet puddings, I prefer the steamed ones myself to the ones boiled in a cloth, spotted dick. Sometimes a bread and butter pudding—a proper one with eggs and currants. Sometimes Mother would say 'I'll make you a Queen of Puddings'. That's with breadcrumbs and jam with meringue on top. My mother didn't make bread or wine, but she made some jam and always cakes.

It was a bit grim in the First War. Rationing did not come in until 1917 but there wasn't much around. We used to have maize pudding I remember. I loved that. My mother made it like rice pudding—yellow stuff. I have never seen it since. Sometimes we might get a rabbit or a few sausages. You bought pork sausages at Mr King's pork shop. He sold only pork products. Pies and salt pork as well as fresh. My mother cooked on a kitchen range—a lovely kitchener it was—and we ate in the same room as we cooked, but it was a proper dining table.

The vegetables and other work was all done there too. There was a copper. We had a sofa in there and my father had an old Windsor chair with arms. If we sat in it we were always turned out 'That's your dad's chair'. We all had our places round the table and the baby was in a high chair. The table was always properly laid with a cloth and the vegetables in dishes and a cruet. I expect they were quite strict about our table manners. We always sat down even at tea-time. After my father died my mother had the kitchener taken out and a fireplace cut in and the room made a very nice dining room. In the last years she lived in the bottom half herself, and let the top which gave her an income to live on.

We never had bathrooms when I was a child—nobody did. We used to have the old hip bath in front of the fire and in your bedroom you had the wash basin and jug, and a slop bucket. All the bedrooms had those. Even after I was married it was still the same, and we used to have a big bungalow bath. After the Second World War we put a bathroom into our house in Salisbury Road, before grants were ever thought of! And that was the first bathroom I ever had.

At the corner of Claremont there was a little cafe, Black Cat Tearooms it was called. It was where Paiges and the little cafe next door are now. The lady who was cook there lived next door to the school and at the end of November 1918 she came in looking for someone to go in the cash desk there. So I went there until April of the next year. By that time it was very quiet in the town, the soldiers had all gone, and Miss Compton asked me if I wanted to go there. That was R.S. Compton in Norman Road where Stuart Horsler is now. A very nice long-established drapers they were, and I stayed there for eight years until I left to get married. I went into the baby linen and underwear department.

Compton's was quite an interesting firm. Miss Compton told me that her parents came from Northampton. They got married in 1874 or 1875 and came down to London. They stopped there long enough to buy some stock and then they came to Hastings and took a draper's shop in the High Street. They found that it was a bit far up the High Street so they moved to the corner of High Street and George Street. I think it is a pie shop now, but for many years it was a draper's shop. Then for a little while they were in York Buildings where Moseleys is today I think. Pearch and Simmons were at 32 and 34 Norman Road, then so the two firms swopped over. Pearch and Simmons went to the High Street and Compton's went to St Leonards. There was a big family of the Comptons but I think they have all died out. There were two sisters who didn't marry. One son went out to India where he had two sons, but when he came back he did not go into the business. And the other son, Mr Ernest, was working for Frank East drapers shop at

Tonbridge. He did come back to go into the business in the thirties but he was asked to return to Frank East and went back as manager. The old governor was a Deacon at Wellington Square Baptist Church. They finally closed down about 1960. I noticed an obituary to one of Compton's staff in the paper recently—Mrs Covey—she was ninety-seven. She started at Compton's on the same day in April 1919 that I did. She was Miss Deeprose then. She was in the millinery department. The obituary said that she was the oldest member of Norman Road Methodist Church.

You always had to ask for a rise in those days—you never just got one—and one time when I asked for a rise they said I could stop to mid-day dinner instead. My mother didn't mind that because I went first party and ate with the governor, and we had beautiful food. You always knew what you were going to have but there was always plenty of it, second helpings if you wanted it. There was a housekeeper and she and the boss sat with us. About three or four of us went. You had three-quarters of an hour, and then a bell rang and the second party came in.

My father was called up 31st August 1916 and he was in the trenches. They used to have a fortnight in the trenches and a fortnight at the base. A group of them was sheltering in a ruined barn on the way back to the trenches and a bomb fell nearby. All the beams fell in and my father was buried—January 1917 that was. So he was sent home with shell-shock. He was forty-one. They said he couldn't do the paperhanging any more, so they gave him a few months' course in electrics and he got a job with Adams and Jarrett. But the other men didn't like it because he wasn't a union man so he was out on the dole. I can remember we had a Mayor's parcel that Christmas. Poor people had a parcel of goodies at Christmas from the Mayor. It was the only year we ever had it. My mother did not like it at all. Eventually my father went back to his old work. He was only sixty when he died in 1935. He had angina, but he never got over the shell-shock.

I can't remember my father helping with household chores, well men didn't in those days. He did the garden. He used to take us out on Sunday afternoons, or evenings in the summer. Those trips were highlights. We used to go to friends in Hollington Old Lane for tea on Sundays—remember that we were down in St Leonards—then we used to go up to the Victoria and sit in the garden and have that lovely gingerbeer. Draught gingerbeer. (I can remember going on a boat trip on the Thames once and stopping at a little riverside place for gingerbeer.) If we didn't go to Hollington then we would go the other way to the Bull. In those days there was a little motor train that went from Bexhill. It always came along at half past nine and you could get on at Glyne Gap, which was what we always did. If you missed it you had to walk home. We were very small at the time. After 1913, when my brother came along, we didn't go out so much. And when the war came it made an awful lot of difference. Well, we were always busy, we had always got people in, and when you live at the seaside, well your relatives find you, don't they?

I can remember Sunday school outings. They used to give us pork pie when we got there for our lunch. It was considered a treat. Usually there would be a tea laid on for us as well at a church hall. We would have games during the day. Once we walked to Camber Castle and it took ages because we were crossing the fields and kept coming to ditches. We were quite big girls then eleven or twelve. It was all wild then. Of course they developed Winchelsea in the twenties and thirties. All those bungalows. And Camber, which is the other side of the river. There used to be a golf course where the holday camp is now. We used to go to Camber Sands. You had to go over the bridge into the camp site and there was a little train, only trucks, that took you all across fields down to Camber Sands for a penny or twopence.

The only job I remember having to do regularly was to polish up Nurse Neill's brass plate out the front. When I got older I liked to do a bit of cooking but no one made me do any jobs. We used to help by looking after the younger ones and we all had a paper rounds. The going rate was about eighteen pence then. I had one before I left school for a shop in Silchester Road. Sanders was the name. I had quite a long round and there were always soldiers who wanted a copy of the paper, but there were never any spare ones so you had to hang on to them which wasn't always easy. I went one night a week as well as the mornings and on Saturday morning I would do a little shopping for Mrs Sanders and for all that I got two and tuppence a week. And during the war we had a very nice couple staying with us. I think the man had joined up as a private, but he had been a solicitor or something like that. They had a little boy and I used to take that child out. Later they moved to Silverhill but I still used to take him out so his mother could go and play cards. They paid me eighteen pence for that. I was very tall and grown up for my age. Even when I started work at Compton's the older ones used to say I didn't seem like an apprentice, because in those days you started off as an apprentice before you became an improver; more like themselves.

We used to have volunteer fire brigades in those days. Both my father and my father-in-law were in it. My father-in-law was station officer at Shepherd Street and lived over the fire station. He went there in 1908 when it was built at the back of the Kinema. He was in it for more than 30 years. My father started as a call boy at fourteen. Call boys had to run down to the garage for the horses and bring them up that steep little side street, Cross Street, by the Old England, to Shepherd Street, before they had Mary. I think they had the first motorised fire engine and they called it Mary after Captain Chesham's wife. And that was garaged in the fire station. Levetleigh was my father's last fire. 1913 that was. My brother was born that night. And it broke out the next night again and my father had to go back. And after that he came out. He was thirty-nine so he had been in for twenty-five years. I have always understood that the Suffragettes were to blame for Levetleigh. It was a lovely house owned by our member of Parliament, Sir Arthur du Cros, on the corner of Dane Road and Brittany Road opposite the Markwick Gardens. It is called Firtree Corners now and there is a bungalow there.

The fire brigade had bells. When the bells rang whatever the men were doing they had to leave to attend the fires. They got paid for the fires. But other than that there were practice nights and cleaning nights. And they always had an outing and perhaps they might be away two nights in Portsmouth for competitions. The paid brigade came in at the end of August 1938. The last fire for the volunteers was Dengate's in Queens Road and it was a big one. It was rather funny really because the paid brigade was there. But it was a day or two before they were due to take over, so the volunteer brigade came and I don't think the paid people felt very friendly to the volunteers. Dengate's was on the corner by the cricket ground of course. I know it was 1938 because my twins were not quite a year old and I remember going down. There were volunteer fire stations all over the town. One up at Silverhill, I think they still call that Corporation Yard, where the bus stop is on to Battle Road. There was one in Bohemia, one in Shepherd Street, another at Mercatoria.

You know the houses at the top of Norman Road with the gardens out the front—when I was a child there were no gardens there—we always referred to that area as 'the gravel'. The backs of those houses overlook the Mercatoria School playground. Those gardens were never fenced off like that until after the First World War. I suppose when people bought the houses they found they owned that bit in front too. When war broke out in 1914 they brought the Welsh Fusiliers and some of the Yorkshiremen and they used to drill on that bit of gravel. I remember that they were territorial units and they had been under canvas on manoeuvres, and they brought them in and billeted them on people all around. It was the end of the letting season and my grandmother had six. And all their muddy blankets and everything! Welshmen and Yorkshiremen.

By 1916 we had the Canadians here and they were billeted in the empty houses. I think that a lot of those big houses round Warrior Square and West Hill were seaside residences of people who had London houses too. They used to come down for holidays and bring all their staff. There used to be a lot of titled people here. After the war they were turned into guest houses. Of course there was quite a lot of empty property before the war. I can remember the Clock House standing empty for years. And Miss Scot used to have a nursing home in what is now St Leonards Rectory, which closed down after the First World War. There were lots of private schools which evacuated and never came back.

I remember at the start of the First War, August Bank Holiday it was, and we had taken our tea on to the beach and there was Aunt Sophie who lived at Redhill and another aunt from Ashford with us. I remember Aunt Sophie who was the funny one of the family saying 'Well if war comes you won't be able to stay here. It won't be safe on the coast!' But we did stay. There was such a difference between the two wars. In the First War the town was buzzing with people all along the seafront, and there were bands. They kept on the summer things you see, it was still like a holiday place. But in the Second War that was all different. I can remember coming back after we had been evacuated—we had been away for only sixteen weeks, but my husband was still earning our living here, so we came back. We always took the children out for a walk on Sunday afternoon and when he asked 'Where shall we go', I said, 'How about along the seafront'. He gave me such a funny look and said 'Well the seafront isn't very healthy these days'. Of course it was all barbed wire along there then. So we had to go out to Church-in-the-Wood—it was all country then. I shouldn't know it now.

STAN MOON

Born 1906

I was born in November 1906 in Stonefield Road, Hastings. My father was a builder and decorator locally. He came down here for his health really, from Dulwich; they were Dulwich builders. As far as I know my grandfather came from Yalding in Kent. But my mother's side were London people, Herne Hill way. There were six boys and one girl in the family. And there was a previous one who died. We had an Olive who was the first, I think, of the family, who we never knew, of course, but they used to tell us about her.

We were quite a big family really, I suppose. But during the War, the First World War, there were eight of us, because my uncle and aunt's children stayed with us. That's my mother's family side. My aunt was munition making, and my uncle was in the Royal Flying Corps, as it was then, the Air Force. They had a boy and a girl, my cousins, and they came to us.

Even with that, as the War came on, they were billeting troops in Hastings from various parts of the country and we had some of them bedded with us. We had four South Wales Borderers. They were lovely chaps, and one of them I remember he had an accordian, which he could play and they would sing. I was only a youngster then, and they had their full kit, and their rifles, everything to go abroad. They all went to Gallipoli and pretty nearly the whole of that lot were killed. They were the finest chaps you could wish to find. I shall never forget that. I used to play with their rifles, I could take a Lee-Enfield to bits, and clean it and I was only nine years old. I had all sorts of various guns—air guns, shot guns and sporting guns, but I never used a .303 rifle until I was in the Police War Reserve, in the War, and we had a range somewhere near Catsfield or Crowhurst. We were all learning to shoot, as they thought, and we went out to this shoot and we had five rounds each. I don't know what the distance was on the range, but I got four bulls and one inner the first time I shot. And another fellow, he got the same score, so they said, 'Well, we'll see who is the best.

You two can have another five rounds each'. So we all put something in the kitty and they had the markers up at either end of the range and I got five bulls. I'd never handled the gun before and I got nine bulls and one inner. That's all through playing with those guns of those soldiers!

I went to school in Clive Vale, round Githa Road. I would be five when I started. I met the headmistress and my teacher, Miss Crowhurst, and the Governess—before Miss Shoesmith—wore a high collar and a long black skirt. I hated school. I'll tell you why. I was all right in the earlier stages. I used to enjoy it and get a prize every year until I got into standard one or two and I had glandular trouble. I had swollen glands in the neck. That was very common in those days and they often would turn tubercular. You often saw a child with a mark, a cut, in the neck where they took the glands out. It used to show where they couldn't stitch it up like they do nowadays. Because I got these swollen glands they suspected TB, and the doctor said 'You'll have to go away'. So I went to Margate Royal Sea Bathing Hospital. I went there for three months during one year, the whole of the summer. And the whole summer again, the next year. So for two years I missed three months schooling. In those days when you went to Clive Vale, or any school, you went standard by standard. What you didn't get in each year you were down in the standard next year. And what did me was fractions and division with arithmetic. Writing; spelling I was always good at. History, scripture; I'd take prizes for that.

They were very, very strict in those days. If you missed one day the school board man was round banging on the door next morning to see your parents and ask why you weren't there. I got half time and I went to work when I was thirteen years old. I went to school in the morning and got off in the afternoon. I went to work for a dairy in Alfred Road. His name was old Jimmy White and he had the old pony and cart. He used to do all the Clive Vale round. I used to have to get up at five o'clock in the morning, be up to Alfred Road by six o'clock on this old pony and cart. An open backed thing, a float, as you'd call it. We used to go right up through Ore, up Fairlight Road right down to Home Farm, Fairlight Place. On the way to Fairlight Glen, right at the bottom there's a private road cuts down to Home Farm. That, I believe, belonged to Sam Mills. We used to have to go down there, and get one lot of milk. All hand stuff in those days, in big churns. They'd stand on the front of the old milk float and then we came back down Fairlight Road down to Tile Kiln Farm, which was Smith's Farm, just at the top end of Fairlight Avenue. Guy Smith had a nice bungalow built on the end of Fairlight Avenue, the corner that faces Fairlight Road and Fairlight Avenue. He was the last one there. He kept a few cows there and carried on for a while until they sold out to build all those houses that are there now. And then after we'd got the milk from the Home Farm and Smith's Farm, we had to come back to start a round and go all round Clive Vale.

It wasn't in bottles. We had hand cans and also small cans; there was half pints, pints, and quart cans and you had your hand can with a half pint measure in it. You put it all in people's jugs that they left at the door, or you left them a can at the door, and you collected all your empty cans. When you finished the round you'd go back to the dairy in Alfred Road and you had to wash, in scalding water, all those cans and their brass handles, and little brass hinges. All that lot had to be clean, and left all ready for the round the next time. And then after that I used to have to go home and have my breakfast and get to school for nine o'clock. That's what I did when I was thirteen and a half years old, and do you know how much I got for that a week? A shilling, and that's seven days a week. I was never given any milk. No free milk, nothing. And the milkmen did an afternoon round, that they used to call the pudding round.

People used to like our milk, rather funny because all the milk was local milk. The other farms were Shearers Farm which someone else ran and Whitemans Farm down Pett. And you know why people used to prefer our milk? We used to slightly colour it. Because when you get milk from the farm it's white as white, white as snow it is, so we used to put a little drop of cochineal in it to give it that lovely rich colour. I expect today they still do that now. No milk is coloured really, except if you get a good Guernsey or a Jersey. My brother Les, he'd been farming for years and years, and I got a bit of experience during part of the War with him rearing dairy stock and everything. We used to keep a Guernsey there to mix with the other milk to colour it up, because it's twice as rich as the average. I did the milk round until I was about fifteen, I suppose. I had half time from thirteen to about fifteen, and then we decided I'd have another job.

Clive Vale was a very classy school locally. Ore and Sandown were the two troubles. I don't remember much about Ore; only the fact that it was in our, sort of, playground area. The old Blacksmith's was behind there where we used to get our iron hoops mended on a

Saturday morning. Two brothers, Easton. It used to cost a penny and that was our pocket money, so we was sunk for the week then. We used to play other games too. For different times of the year, we did different sorts of things, you know, from nowadays.

When we were doing hoops all these girls had these diablos. Diablos are a kind of spinning top. They had two sticks with a string on them and they used to keep these going, and shoot them right up in the air, and run them down the street. Some were so good. There was that Doris Hook, used to be living at the bottom of Athelstan Road. She was a champion. Lovely girl, lovely black curly hair, and rosy face. She used to get it, work it up to speed, she'd send it right up, over the tramwires, and catch it the other side and run it down the string. Marvellous!

Opposite the old Blacksmith's in Ore, which is a key shop now, there was an old lady, a very old lady. The place was so stuffy it used to hit you when you opened the door. Miss Playford, her name was. Well she used to sell kites for a penny. They were made of coloured paper, blues and greens and that, and they had a little thin cane frame. But you couldn't fly it till you'd made a tail. So we used to get all bits of newspaper and bits of string to make a tail to balance it up, and then get out and do them in Harold Road till they got caught up. So Saturday afternoon, there's this series of coloured kites hanging up top till they eventually got cut off with the overhead tram doings.

Good Friday was skipping rope day, and all our aunts, uncles, and grannies used to come, and we'd have Mum's clothes-line right across the road and the aunts and uncles used to turn it and the children would go through it and jump in and out. The only time we stopped was when Mr Lindridge came down with his milk float. We used to drop the rope down and he'd go over it. Unless a horse and cart came by. Course, there were no cars then.

I don't remember moving to Clive Vale, I just remember being there. When we moved to Athelstan Road a family called Spiers were our next door neighbours. They had a laundry next door to us and they had no main water. As you opened our back door their back door was just there, and they had a well there. All the water for washing all the laundry had to be got up by hand from the well. So, long before daybreak, you heard this great bucket clattering down into the well, and they'd wind it up, and down it'd go, while they was filling big tubs and things for this laundry to work for the day. I don't know how they heated it. There was several women worked there, you know, and of course, they were all shouting when they started out. There was no peace.

There was a pond over the back of our house. We used to go and buy watercress there. The pond was between Edwin Road and Athelstan. He was a dairyman. We used to go and get a pennyworth of pears over there. We could go from our garden through to his garden. We'd have a big overcoat on, and we'd buy our pears up at the house, and as we came back we used to pick up and fill our coat pockets full as we came through the orchard. We could hardly walk in our garden path for pears.

In the Harold Road shops just above the two reservoirs, there's always been a shop there where you could buy bottles of pop for a penny, with the old marble in the top. Well, for a penny you could buy a fishing line complete with its line, bobber and hook. All we had to do was go over the fields, the Ressies fields we used to call them. And that was our playground for lots of things. We could cut a stick off one of the trees and when they weren't looking, hop over the fence (the gate was locked and you couldn't get in) and do a little bit of fishing till the old gamekeeper came along from Fairlight and used to chase us out. All sorts of things we could get up to over there. Then we had those fields where they built those houses behind from Belmont Road, comes right down to Gurth Road and all through there. That was our area, we all congregated and played all the summer in those fields.

When the summers were long and warm and we had our usual month's holiday, we used to get boards and when the grass got dry we used to slide down those banks, right down those fields as if we was on snow. And in the winter time we used big old tea trays as toboggans. We couldn't afford sledges, or anything like that. And all those fields, they used to come right from the top of Barley Lane right down to the reservoir fences. There was a farm there, actually, called Jupp's Farm. So we used to use that as a wintertime sport. You know, we always had something to do.

Course, nobody could ever afford a bike. If you went down Rock-a-Nore over the tip, where everything was shot over there, you'd find old bicycle wheels with half the spokes missing or an old frame. We used to get them, and get a bit of old iron, a bit of old poker, and tie a piece of sacking over where the saddle was, and we used to go over one field on the left hand reservoir as you face it—it's difficult to describe because they've built over it now—well we had a long run down there and we'd take these old bikes, with the old wheels scraping on the side of the forks. If you rode it too much you used to cut through your forks till your forks would drop off. Anyway, you'd get on and see if you could stick on this thing and come right down these banks to the bottom, still sitting on. We used to thoroughly enjoy it, that was a good sport for a long time.

I had half time at school between about thirteen and fifteen, and we decided I ought to get another job. I started on a firm of builders from Bexhill; our namesake, but I don't know if they're any relation at all, a firm of Moon and Gardeners. They owned all of Dorset Road, Bexhill. They'd built it actually, years and years ago, and they still had nearly all the property. The upper part was mainly high class girls' schools. There were two parts, Upper Dorset and Lower Dorset Road, so we maintained all of Lower Dorset Road. I got ten shillings a week. I used to catch the bus, the tram, at the Memorial, at seven o'clock to get over to Bexhill. It used to cost me sixpence a day return, on the old iron tram. It used to take half an hour to get there. I used to get there and walk down to our workshops in Manor Lane, off Manor Road. It's all been built on now. I used to get home about seven o'clock.

I didn't do an apprenticeship as such, not a signed apprenticeship. I was there as just a beginner. We did all the repairs and what have you, so I was with all the various tradesmen, always the boy, the labourer, so I learned an awful lot. Didn't have much time for hobbies. The first time I started real fishing was with my father when I'd started work. I'd be about fourteen or fifteen, and if we had a nice day in the autumn he'd say 'Well, this afternoon we'll go fishing'. Opposite the cinema you could hire boats by the hour for fishing. They'd supply handlines and lugworms and all that sort of thing, and we'd have two or three hours fishing. We'd row off behind what we used to call the Cinema Rocks, a big shoal of rocks in front of the cinema in those days. Not Castle Rocks but inside that lot. They've all disintegrated and worn away now. They were quite huge then. We'd go off, perhaps, at one o'clock and come back about four, just before dusk, at November time when the fish were here, and we used to get as much fish as we could carry up the beach. It was so plentiful. They were all whiting and dabs, that sort of thing. It was marvellous then.

Of course, there wasn't any trawling or trammel netting, anything like that in those days. The trawlers were there, but they used to go off for the week. They wouldn't trawl inshore. They'd got to make it pay, and work hard. They used to go to Rye Bay, one good fishing area here. The Diamonds was another good one, way out off Hastings, about twelve to fourteen mile out, something like that. There was various fishing grounds where they knew more or less what they were going to get, that time of year. They worked hard, and then came back in, in their great big old leather sea boots.

In about 1924 we moved to Kent House, from Athelstan Road, and then High Street.

My father had a lot more work, and was getting busier; so he asked if I'd leave Bexhill and come with him. So I went with him until the time he died. So we was in the High Street. Old Taggy was our neighbour, the old musician, old Lex Tagger with his walking stick and his bowler hat. He used to hit his head with his walking stick, like this, on his head. Hard as iron. He'd bang his head just to show what he could do. You try it, you wouldn't do it again. And he often used to wear a big sombrero, or a bowler, one of the old bowlers. And as soon as he got that bowler on we used to come up behind and give him a bash on the top and dent his bowler right in. He used to take it in good faith. He was a marvellous neighbour. He could play any instrument. I'll tell you what his full time job was, he used to give lessons in his house, and sold instruments, and that. He was in the old Gaiety Theatre orchestra. He used to play the violin.

In different districts they had soup kitchens. One of them was All Souls, in their parish room in Athelstan Road; one was down in All Saints Street where the Fishermens Institute is now. They used to make huge quantities of soup. Anybody that hadn't got a meal could take their big jug up there, and get it filled with soup. A lot of them had to rely on that.

I know that we had one or two children that came up from All Saints Street that really should have gone to All Saints Street School. They never had any boots on and they were sent to school for the day with no food. And the boys that stayed to dinner used to have sandwiches that we brought, and each boy would give a bit of his dinner to these poor children. There was some really poor families around.

The Old Town wasn't quite so poor in the 1920s. You had a good brewery in the Old Town. Breed's Brewery. And various things were going which employed quite a bit of labour; and the fishing was all very good and they were growing. They'd got bigger boats, better boats, they'd got engines and they could get further afield, get more fish in. We lived very comfortably. I suppose the average wages there was about two pounds fifteen shillings to three pounds a week.

There was one long bad spell, I suppose that'd be the General Strike, 1926. I know it's the quietest time I remember. My dad had died and I was running the business. We employed a regular carpenter, old Archie Hayward, and we didn't have enough work even to keep him going. For the first week or two we made odd steps and repaired this and that, but that's the only time I can remember that things got really and truly quiet. But I can't say that anyone went short, not really short.

Some of the places in George Street I remember like the printers. I worked in there. As a boy I went in there with the old plumber who was working with us then, to repair a burst underneath the floor. He was a miserable old so-and-so. He committed suicide, eventually. And I'll tell you where his workshop was, of all places. It's now called the Piece of Cheese. Look at the fuss they've made of it; an old historic this, that and the other. It was just the end of a terrace. It was a half a house, a little wedge, so later on someone had a bright idea and called it a piece of cheese. But it was a plumber's workshop and this old boy committed suicide in his workshop, in it.

Also in George Street was Barnes's rag and bone yard. Full of rats, rabbit skins, empty bottles. If you came through George Street there was Barnes's there, they used to put all their rabbit skins down underneath to dry. You can imagine what that was like in the middle of the summer. That was when you got into George Street. So you held your breath when you got into George Street. And you held your breath till you got to the end of George Street, took a deep breath because in West Street there was Blissards' melting all the fat down from all the cattle offal all night, so all that stench was coming out, and you ran as quick as you could past there, took a good deep breath before you go to Roebuck Yard to get by Verrells's yard, till you got a bit of clear air at the top of the High Street.

I remember election time, sort of. We didn't really know what it was all about, just some kind of local fever that had got up. I remember one irate Labour chap called Jimmy Cox, he used to shout the odds on the beach every night trying to persuade everybody to adopt socialism—it was the finest thing in the world. Eustace Percy was another one. First Sunday in the month, the Councillors used to go up to the morning service at St Clement's Church. We used to shout, 'Here comes Ali

Hastings visitors

Baba and the forty thieves'.

What you could buy with a penny though! Opposite Miss Clark's, the printers, was our best sweet shop where we could go on our way to the cinema where you used to get in for a penny on a Saturday afternoon, up in the gods. And everybody used to take in peanuts. And we sat on hard benches. Maxwell's was the sweet shop. And we had a packet of chocolates, four ounces a penny, and he had all slab toffee in tin trays, four ounces a penny. Greengage, strawberry, raspberry, all sorts of various ones. And you used to go in for a pennyworth of toffee and you'd pick up the doings and slap, slap, slap, clatter, clatter, clatter; and he had these tongs that break it up into smaller pieces. They'd last you all the afternoon. Scorched peas you could get too, in the Tudor House there, 58 and 59 All Saints Street. They were pidgeon peas, field peas, and they baked them. You used to get hard 'uns and soft 'uns. They used to fill your pocket; straight into your pocket. We used to go to school with them, so if you got caught in school, eating scorched peas, you had to go in front of the class, and take all your scorched peas out and put them all in the wastepaper. They were lovely. But what we used to like later on was roasted peanuts. In the shuck. In All Saints Street. Mrs Richardson.

And there was Joe Mamone who used to stand at the other end of George Street, with his chestnuts. He had lovely hot baked and buttered potatoes, salted and peppered, and baked chestnuts all going in this great big coke fire. We used to get them when we came out of the cinema. He was quite a character. And he used to sell icecream over on the beach 'Okey cokey penny a lump'.

Later, I went to evening school, even after I'd finished school. Old Dickie Dermott was my teacher. What we did to him once, he used to wear a hard bowler hat always. Well, when he went out to the lav once we took his hat and screwed it to the bench and filled it with shavings.

And Biddy the Tubman. I knew him for years. He was a fisherman by day. And then there was the Sand Scratcher that used to do the drawings in the sand. He was a marvellous artist; drew huge pictures. He had just like a gardening tool and as the tide went out on a summer's day he used to set to work and do, perhaps, Hastings Castle, and people would throw their coppers over as they went by. And there used to be a nice military band in the summer, opposite the White Rock. Then you had the old Punch and Judy show a bit further along.

MARY HILL

Born 1906

I was born at Scrivens Building in the Old Town. My father was a
fisherman and a lifeboat man. My mother worked as a cook in a hotel.
There were nine of us altogether, and another one who died at birth. I
was seventh.

We lived in the house I was born in for twelve years and then we
moved to Tackleway, and then to All Saints Street. I stopped there
until I was married to Bill and we came to Ore then. Done all our
courting under the old round Fishmarket.

I was thirty-four when my father died. He lived to a good age. We
had to look after ourselves when our mother was at work; went hungry
sometimes. It was very bad in the fishing days then. When there was no
fish there was no money because there was no dole, nothing like that.
We used to go down the soup kitchen and get a pennorth of soup in a
jug, but before that we went to school, because my mother was out to
work. My parents didn't live together all that many years before they
parted. My father loved his drink, he used to go and have his pint. But
Mum, she never drank. I can't remember them much being at home.

It was a hard life and we often went to school with no breakfast, but
if we went to school early every morning, at the end of the week we
was granted a little brass disc to go to the breakfast room. That was
down under the fisherman's place that is now, in All Saints Street.
There used to be a soup kitchen underneath there. We went there for
breakfast and one morning we'd have bread and milk and a piece of
bread and jam, and the next morning we had porridge and a piece of
bread and dripping. That was our breakfast so we wouldn't go to
school hungry.

The school board man. We used to be frightened to death of the
school board man if you stopped away from school. And he used to
stand watching us 'Eat that' so that you ate it all up. And if there was a
lump in the porridge some of the boys would throw it under the table
and he used to nab them for it too. But we looked forward to those

breakfasts too. It really was hunger sometimes there. It was all the Old Town. Well some wasn't so bad off as that. Well I won't say more.

I went to All Saints School at first, the infants in All Saints Street, and then I went to Waterloo School in Waterloo Passage in All Saints Street. It leads down into the Bourne. I was three when I first went to school. I can't remember how big the classes were. All I can remember, and this is going right back, I remember the coronation of the old King and Queen, and we was presented with a mug. I wish I'd saved it because it would have been worth a lot of money. And also I remember an election going on and I can remember us singing, 'Vote, vote, vote for Mr du Cros. Throw old Johnson in the sea'. But what their politics were I don't know! That was in the infant school.

I liked school. I loved scripture. I got a prize for scripture. For punishment at school you would get a whack across the knuckles with the cane, not very vicious, or hold you hand out, but the only thing was they'd shut you in the empty room and leave you there. That was a bit frightening, you was made to stay there. But I never remember the punishments being severe. It was very cold in the winter in the classrooms. No heating then.

I was fourteen when I left school and I went straight into service and got two shillings and sixpence a week. I did scrubbing and housework and that. In a private house in Milward Road it was. I don't think that I wanted to stay on at school. I can't remember wanting to stay on. I wasn't very good at arithmetic. I was good at scripture, I suppose, as I was saying, and also I was good at writing essays, compositions and that, but arithmetic I was awful at it, no good at all.

I had a part time job at school. I'd be about twelve or thirteen then. It was in the fish shop in All Saints Street, for Mr and Mrs Gallop and I used to skin the fish. They was the flaps. I don't suppose they save them now, the breast part. But they was ever so sweet. Beautiful fish it was.

We might have a penny for pocket money now and again. You can't really remember such things as that. But I took bottles and jars, and bones. We used to go along to Rock-a-Nore and pick up the old bones and take them along to Verrells in the Bourne. And cinders we used to get to make a fire. Because sometimes you'd be without a fire. We used to go along the groyne and pick the cinders, because they used to empty the dustcarts over there then. We used to bank up a fire with them or burn what we could of them, old boots, anything we could to make a bit of heat.

I used to go the Ragged School, what they call the Ragged School, in Tackleway. It was a Sunday school. From there once a month we used to go to All Saints Church for the service. I used to love that. We went to the Sunday school down the Bourne as well, in the Bourne Mission, Band of Hope in the Crown Lane. When we went on a treat, I remember that we went to Ore valley, and I thought we'd gone miles. We went up in, I think it was a tram. We thought it was wonderful, because we had games and races. And tea. That was the main thing, the food. And oranges. I don't remember going anywhere else.

Some people thought they were better than us. Shan't say their name. I don't want to give anything away, but they always thought they were better than us, because they was all dressed nicely. To be quite truthful you envy them, don't you when they're dressed in nice clothes and that. We just thought they looked down on us then.

The house in Providence Row they've pulled down now. There was just the kitchen we called it then, and the bedrooms, no sitting room. Two bedrooms and an attic at the top. And then the house in Tackleway, that was a very old house and that had just the kitchen, because there were no sitting rooms in those days, and the two bedrooms and the attic at the top. I slept in a bed with my sister. There were just us two in the bedroom. My brothers they was all upstairs. No baths—a tin bath in front of the fire. You just washed in the handbasin. There was no water in the house. It was out in the yard and you had to carry it from there up into the house. We cooked on a stove—just an ordinary stove—fire stove—fire grate that's all. And the gas was a jet, I remember now—of course we had lamps—but the gas was a jet. Just a bare light—no mantle.

In the winter, of course, we hadn't got any bedclothes there. Sometimes it was old coats and that. We used to go to the vicarage, All Saints, and we used to borrow blankets to put on the bed and then you used to take them back at the end of the winter. That used to help us out. I shouldn't want my childhood back again! No I don't!

Two blind men, and they used to be outside Caroline Parade outside the Chatsworth Hotel, and they had this piano on a cart like and one had a violin, and they used to play beautifully. All these songs. They were two brothers. Both blind. People used to stop and listen and they were there for a good many years, and made quite a living out of it. They were two beautiful players. And there was the Punch and Judy man, of course. They were on the beach. My uncle, father's brother, he was a shoeblack right opposite where the old Albertine used to be, the big boat. And in All Saints Street the old barrel organ, Tony Mear, used to come and we used to dance, in the road. I can never remember not being able to dance. I could always dance. When we were little kids we used to dance to this barrel organ.

At school we played skipping, and hopscotch, and tag as they called it. Marbles of course. I didn't belong to any organisations, but we did have a pet, a dog, little captain. A mongrel of course, but he was more like a poodle, one of those curly dogs. We used to play more than anything on the beach. We used to play shops on there. Well we had no toys in those days.

There was hardly a Christmas for us like they have now. I remember the first doll I ever had and it was when we was in Tackleway. My mother went along to Jepsons in Robertson Street on Christmas Eve just before they shut, and she bought up some broken toys and took them home. She got a doll for me and a doll for my sister. She put them together—their legs had got broken—and she dressed them. She was up until two o'clock in the morning doing it. My sister had a doll with a wax face and a sawdust body. She dressed them as Red Riding Hoods. There was only that one toy we had and I remember so plainly, there was an old wicker arm chair by my bed and my doll was sitting in it, and when I saw it, oh it was wonderful. And my sister she loved hers, but we took them to bed with us that night and of course she laid on her doll, didn't she, and it had a wax face, and it 'codsed' it all, bless her. But she loved it just the same.

POLLY MEPHAM

Born 1910

I was born January 10th 1910 in Clive Vale, Hastings. We moved to East Grinstead when my dad got a job bricklaying, and then we came back when the First World War broke out. So we must have lived up there two or three years. And when we came back here we lived down Percy Road. I lived there until I got married.

I had one sister and two brothers. Albert was the youngest, he was killed in Tunisia. Then there was Fred who died when he was fifty-four, and then my sister Anne, she died at sixty-three. So now there's only me. My father was sixty-eight when he died. He was a bricklayer but when he lost his leg in the First World War he just took up anything he could make a living off. He built these houses. Then he used to sweep chimneys. Anything to earn a shilling or two. When he first came out of the army, he used to buy these old fashioned carriages take the wheels off and build these two wheel cart things, and traders used to buy them off him to sell their goods from, like fish or vegetables. He did all sorts of jobs after he couldn't do the building. You know at the top of Fairlight Road where there is a little pond, where you go down to the Glen opposite the Glen gate, there used to be a seat and he used to have a barrow there and sell fruit, oranges and bananas. He had a big thing he made lemonade in, and glasses, and my mum used to wash out the glasses. Used to sell lemonade up there twopence a glass. And bananas. He had a chameleon in one of these boxes of bananas. He took it over one of the schools to find out what it was, if it was dangerous, and it was a chameleon, one of those things that change colour. Anyway we left it over there, let them have it. We didn't want it.

My mother went out to work when the First World War was on with Aunt Nell, her sister. They used to do the laundry. They used to take it off the hospitals. And she used to do the washing and Aunt Nell used to do the ironing. She didn't do no more when Dad came out of the army. Only hop picking, the usual thing you used to do.

When we went hop picking we went in the wagon. Used to pile a tea chest in with all the odds and bobs whatever you was taking. They was long wagons with side bits and the kids and people used to sit all on the sides there and all the traps was in the middle. And we used to sing on the way there. It was great fun. I remember hop picking with an umbrella, you'd pick so many a day. Used to have to get on with it too. We slept out there once at Sempstead Farm at Ewhurst. There was a whole row of new huts he'd got there—they was nice. They'd built racks up over the beds to put whatever on. They was quite cosy, those little huts. At the bottom there was like a galvanised top and they used to make this bonfire out of a big pile of faggots and you used to bake potatoes and all in that. We used to bake potatoes and sit round the fire singing in the evenings.

First day we got there my Albert went and climbed up a crab apple tree and fell down, we thought he'd killed hisself. He'd knocked hisself out, but he was all right, bit bruised. We did enjoy it in them days. We didn't have holidays. For cooking you just had a campfire. You had a long piece with a hook on and you boiled your billycan on that to make tea. And you had a couple of bricks, put your saucepans on the bricks and built your fire up round them. And you could make a meat pudding and put it on in there. Took a long time to cook when you were hungry and wanted it! There was plenty of water for washing but we used to go home weekends and do more shopping and washing. And for lavatories, you know where you had to go, down in the woods somewhere!

I went to school at Ore Village. I remember the first time. Mrs Austin the governess, took me in. We started at three years old. You left at five years old and went up into the other Ore school. That little school there, that was the infant school until you were five years old. On the right hand side of the track. It's still there. Then you went round to the front side to the other school. The teachers was quite good, a Miss Free, and the governess at the big school was Hunter, Fanny Hunter, and a Miss Miller, and a Miss Polston. If you was naughty Miss Polston would give you the cane. She was one for the cane. None of the others didn't. She stood me over by the grate once. I pushed the thing down and went home. And my mum went up there. But she wasn't the only one. Dolly Coleman, her mother took her up to see the school board man who used to be up Halton. Anyway, she got sacked, because she marked us a lot. It was a different way of teaching

Polly

wasn't it? Stayed in a class for a year, then moved up to the next one,
not changing class every half hour like they do now. You were in class
two for a year then you went up to class three, and class four. And if
you didn't get on you was left down in that class. It was the same
teacher, you got on. I stayed on there until I left school at fourteen and
went into service. I wouldn't have liked to stay on longer at school.
Blow school!

I didn't like service a lot. They've pulled the house down now. She
was very, very old, this lady, Mrs Graves. The poor old gardener, she
used to make him come in and she'd want different things from the
garden when they wasn't even in season. And in bad weather, he'd
have to climb the ladder and talk to her through the windows. Funny
old days they were. I earned eight bob. That was all you got. Eight
shilling. Still you got your food. But you had to be up at six o'clock in
the morning. Do the breakfast room grate and light the fire and then
go in the kitchen—a kitchener there was great old thing—you used to
have to clean the stove and light that fire, and get the breakfast
cracking—get the kettle on. She did have a gas stove in the scullery,
but most of it was done in the kitchen range. And then you'd have to
have the breakfast, then you'd have your breakfast she'd cook it. They
come from New Zealand to look after her. One went back as her father

was ill, and Florrie came to look after the old lady. But they had to take her away in the end. She pulled all her hair out one day. She went properly up the creek you know. So they had to sign and put her away, poor old thing.

I didn't have a part time job to do while I was still at school, but we all had our jobs to do at home. My Fred had to do the fire in the morning, because Mum used to go to work in the morning, and I used to do the shopping. Up the village to Mays the butchers and get meat. Ann used to have to go right down Castle Hill to get the bread from the day before because you got it cheaper—take a sack and get the bread. Of course Albert was little, he didn't have to do anything. On Saturdays we all had our jobs. I used to have to clean the knives with brick dust and shine them up. And we used to have white sort of seated chairs, and we used to have to take them out the back and scrub the seats as white as a pastry board. She would have it done properly. And Ann used to have to scrub the kitchen table. And my Mum used to do the floors. And she'd do her washing on Sunday morning.

The house. Well there was three bedrooms, a sitting room, a kitchen they call it now, we used to call it a scullery and in the corner was the copper which used to burn all the old rubbish, all the old worn out shoes, and boil up your washing in. She had to get the water hot, then she would scrub all that in a tub, then boil it, two or three rinses, then out the back to the mangle and that was the washday. Don't have it easy like they do now. Yes we had a tap. Didn't have no wells, not down Percy Road! We used to have water, but in the winter it used to freeze all over. We used to have to put paraffin on a big piece of rag on a stick, light a match and thaw it out.

She used to cook on an open range at first. What do they call 'em? Ducks nest, with an oven each side, and she used to cook everything on that. It was oil lamps and just the range. (That was up until when we got married and went down there. We had the front room and the middle bedroom. And we had the gas stove put in and the electric light. I think we had the gas light at first. Then we had that taken out and the electric put in.)

No, I didn't belong to any clubs, or Band of Hope. There was nothing like that going, not to my knowledge. You just made your own amusements. Stayed indoors and played ludo. I liked sewing, used to cut up hats and make slippers for the family. We always had a dog, we were never without a dog. Nearly everybody had dogs those days.

Never went fishing, never knew what fishing was. Used to go over the Glen and get winkles. We never had pocket money. Might have got ha'penny now and again if we went shopping. Ha'porth of peanuts or tiger nuts, or what were they called, fried peas, Mrs Law used to have 'em in the village. Used to get a bag of greasy peas all fried for ha'penny.

I used to go to Sunday school. One at Grove Road we used to go. If you went on an outing you took your own cup and saucer, and a bun, kind of thing! We went on a boat. Can't remember where it was now. I know I lost me shoes! It was from the pier somewhere. We didn't pay—it must have been some form of outing.

I remember going over my grandmothers in New Road when Olive Kent was born—that was my father's sister's baby. That was the first baby I'd seen. She was bathing it. I can remember my mother's mother, Mrs Scrace. I can remember Uncle Jim. Harry, he used to have a bit of a wall eye. He used to make a lot of fishing nets. He used to sit and make shrimp nets. My grandmother lived in Percy Road. My Gran used to come over every day when my Mum was working during the war and cook our dinner. Then, when my Gran was ill she lived in my Mum's front room for a while—she was eighty.

My parents had good friends. Old Jack Peters, they used to come up and play dominoes. And Mrs Lloyds. They used to go over there, whatever games they'd got. All the neighbours was open houses then. We always had plenty of people. They used to go to point-to-point meetings—he used to like the fox hounds—go and watch the meetings. Apart from that they didn't do a lot. Went to London now and again to see Ann when she lived up there. Nothing much exciting happened in them days for them. We didn't fly here, there and everywhere.

WINNIE BROAD

Born 1911

I was born on 27th July 1911 in Hastings Old Town. Then I moved to Clive Vale and after that to Barley Lane.

I was married in 1930 and I had six brothers and sisters. My sister Mabel is eighty-three and my sister Elsie is coming up to eighty, then my brother Ike is two years younger, then I come in the middle, two years less, then there's my brother at Wolverhampton. My youngest brother died in the war. My father died in 1918 when he was forty five. He was self employed as a greengrocer. He had a shop in Clive Vale. Mother and father went out together in a horse and cart selling, mostly in St Leonards. My sister, being the eldest, looked after the family, got them to school and all that. I went to Clive Vale School. My father left the shop down Harold Road in the charge of a young lad of about eighteen. He employed him to look after the shop. My brother helped in the shop before and after school. We all had to. My father was never unemployed. He was wrapped up in his work, well he had to be to keep the family going, as there was no other money coming in at all, only what they earned. After he died my mother carried on the same with the horse and cart.

Before my mother married she was a housemaid at the Hydro, which is now Sacred Heart Convent. Then she married at Emmanuel Church, in grey silk and carried those white pom pom flowers.

I can just about remember my father's funeral. He died in 1918 and I can remember the horse carriage coming outside the house and we all went to the cemetery in little black and white gingham dresses, three girls. Mum bought the material in Avery's for sixpence a yard, and we had three made the same and black bows in our hair. I was only eight. And the boys were dressed for the occasion.

When my father died we moved to Barley Lane and lived in a small cottage, two bedrooms, living room, kitchen, back yard with an outside loo. We all slept there, Mum and the two girls in one room and the boys in the other. We had no electricity. Mum had to cook on an open range until my eldest brother paid to have gas put in, gas cooker and gas lights otherwise we had candles and paraffin lamps and that was about 1920 when that was put in. We spent some lovely times there. It was very small but we were all very close. We had no bathrooms only a big bath which hung in the yard, and we took it in turns having a bath in front of the open fire, we had to boil up the water on the open stove. We had a copper in the yard and we boiled the washing and the water in it, and we would get up at six or seven o'clock to get the copper going, we had a tap in the yard which froze up every winter.

We rented our house from a lady at Fairlight for four shillings a week. When my mother died it had gone up to seven shillings and sevenpence a week after she had lived there forty years. The rent was collected by one of the other tenants in the row and he sent it on to the owner. My mother belonged to a benevolent society to pay doctor's fees. My mother had to have parish relief for each child until they reached fourteen, when they left school, and it stopped. They would come and look round your house to see if there was anything you didn't need and they never thought you was entitled to the ten shillings. A Mr Christmas used to come. He lived in Clive Avenue near the pub.

On birthdays we might have a little extra treat, Mum might have bought us a cake, we never had a party or had children round like they do today.

The only musical instrument we had was a 'His Master's Voice' gramophone with a horn to it and winder and six records, one of them was 'The Laughing Policeman'. After that Mum had the piano we all tried to have a go at it.

Once we went to Maidstone Zoo with a singing club Mum had joined us in. We went to All Saints Sunday school outing to Battle once and to Crowhurst. On a picnic outing we went by bus or tram. Mother always took us to the Ebenezer Chapel in Ebenezer Road. We had to go to Sunday school as Mr Morgan lived opposite us. He was our Sunday school teacher, he kept an eye on us as we didn't have a father. He had a lovely big garden, and if we behaved ourselves we were allowed to pick up the windfalls.

We had a lot of friends we played with. Our next door neighbour had three girls and two boys, and the other side there was one son. We played cards, snakes and ladders. We had the open field next to us to play ball games on. We played with skipping ropes and hoops. We played out a lot, only going in when we were hungry. We used to go fishing at the fish ponds at Fish Ponds Farm over Fairlight way. I went with my brothers, and we would take a meal with us and catch a few tiddlers. Mum always had a cat, we always had cats to keep down the mice, they came from the chickens and the slaughter house in the field at the back of our house, although we never saw any.

My two brothers belonged to All Souls Scouts, but I didn't belong to anything. If we behaved we got sixpence a week pocket money each. If we wanted anything else we collected jam jars and took them back and got a halfpenny each for them. We collected enough to take us to the pictures. That was fourpence. That was the only way we made any money. Sometimes we found a golf ball and we would sell it back to the golfers for sixpence.

I can just remember my youngest brother being born. It was 1918, the year my father died. He was three months old when my father died. I can remember because the old nurse that came to deliver him was also attending my Dad in the same room. She used to come up from the Old Town, a sweet old lady carrying a white apron under her arm. Ten shillings for delivering the baby. At the same time she would wash my father and make him comfortable and see to Mum as well.

I can remember my Granny Cheal, she lived in Milward Road. We used to go to see her every Sunday morning. She was in her nineties when she died in Rye.

There was class distinction at school because some of the children were very specially dressed. When it came to me I had to wear my oldest sister's left offs. I can always remember going to a May Day dance round the maypole in the school playground; and I had to wear my sister's dress with a big hem at the bottom. It was in pale blue and I think I was the only one in blue and all the others were in white and I went home and cried my eyes out.

I liked going to school though I wasn't very brainy. I started at four. I often had my knuckles rapped for silly things really, like talking in school or being late or doing something silly. If we didn't go the school board man came after us. We played netball and stoolball in the playground. We did needlework, reading, writing and cooking lessons. I wasn't bad at that. We had to take the ingredients and then would bring home soup in a jam jar. My brothers use to call it anything bar soup, and pastries, all quite simple things, nothing exotic.

I left school at fourteen. Then I went to work at Elphinstone Road as a housemaid, and I used to walk from Barley Lane. I used to get five shillings a week. I got there at nine and worked round to lunch, and they would give me lunch and I would get home about two, so I was gone all morning. I left because the man died and the housekeeper sold the house. Then I went into private service for Mr and Mrs Hocking, who was then Alderman Hocking. I wasn't very happy there. She lost her temper and threw a saucepan at me. Well, my sister worked for Dr. Larkin in Wellington Square as a cook/housemaid, and she was very happy there. I used to go and help with bridge parties because they were connected. One day she came and found me crying and said 'You're not staying there having saucepans thrown at you', so I left and decided to go into hotels where there is more money, twelve shillings a week plus tips.

The first hotel I went to was the Bella Vista in Cambridge Gardens and I stayed there. That's where we went macintosh bathing. We put our swimming costumes on in the hotel and our macintoshes over, took a towel and ran down as quick as lightning to the sea, had a good dip and then back to the hotel ready for work. We started work at seven am, and I wore blue and white in the morning as a chambermaid and in the afternoon I was dressed in black and white as a waitress. I worked from seven till ten for twelve shillings a week plus tips, and one Sunday in two and one half day off a week. Most of the hotels I worked at didn't have running water in their bedrooms like they have today or wash basins, it was all jugs and basins. You had to fill the jugs with hot water from the bathrooms. There wasn't a bathroom to each floor but only two or three to each hotel. The basins had to be cleaned. There were coal fires in the sitting rooms, they all had to be done. Trays taken up to the rooms, shoes to be taken down to be cleaned by one of the porters. You had to collect and take them down and make sure you didn't take them back to the wrong bedroom numbers. You had to do all that as well as make the beds and collecting the trays and bringing them down, and another thing if you were hungry which you sometimes were, we used to take the toast from the trays and take it in the cupboard to eat. The food was all right and if you were off any evening you would come back and find your supper on a hot plate, that is if you wanted it. Before breakfast you had the dining room tables to lay up before the visitors came down, and then when the visitors were having their breakfast we were upstairs making the beds and doing the bedrooms. I had as many as twelve bedrooms to do. Make the beds, empty the slops. Most times the housekeeper would help with the beds but leave you to do the rooms. The better rooms were on the lower floors, we had a lot of bank clerks on the top floor of one hotel.

We had some quite good fun between ourselves. If a woman visitor came in with a fancy hat on we would try it on when they weren't looking.

The porter used to make sure you were in on time at night otherwise he would lock you out. Many times I would walk back home to my Mum because I couldn't get in. Wally got me home late gone ten o'clock and the door was locked, so we walked back and threw a stone up at Mum's window. Usually three girls shared a room at the top of the hotel.

After I left the Bella Vista I went to the Greeba Hotel which was on the sea front by the Palace Pier, and from there I went to the Westgarth Hotel where I married my husband. I was twenty when I got married in 1930. My husband was working at the Queen's Hotel with my brother and I went to visit my brother and saw Wally, we made a date and we courted until we got married a year later. We lived at St Leonards, 70 Norman Road, in a flat at first, then we moved to Alfred Street, St Leonards, where Rita was born. Then we moved to Clive Vale. We never like living in St Leonards.

When we were courting we walked on the hills, or if we went to the pictures we paid between us. Wally and I we used to go to the Kinema which was in Norman Road, St Leonards, or to the Cinema de Luxe. We got a bag of sticky sweets next door for fourpence. On special occasions we would go to the White Rock, because Wally was keen on classical music. We had to save up for that as it cost more money, no we didn't have much time for clubs we just did our courting the cheap way out.

ROSE EDMONDS

Born 1912

I was born in 1912 at 9 School Road, Ore. I lived there from the time I was born until the time I was married in 1934. My maiden name was Cornford.

I had two brothers and one adopted brother. One brother is older than me, he is seventy-five. The younger brother is seventy and the adopted brother died young. My father was about twenty-four when I was born. After the First World War he was out of work for a long time. Then he worked on building and from there he went to the Gas Company and he stayed there until he retired. My mother was twenty-one when I was born. After she was married, she worked at a boarding house down the Croft. I used to go on Saturdays and earned sixpence. My grandmother, who lived next door, looked after the children while she was at work.

I went to Sandown School until I was thirteen and then I went to Priory Road School because the schools changed. I left school when I was fourteen and I worked down Elphinstone Road in a house. I got three shillings for three mornings doing housework. And then I left there and got another job in a laundry to earn more money. I got six pence a week and I still went on Monday and got sixpence and my mother did the other two days. I worked in the laundry until I was married. In the laundry I worked on the callendar at first and then I went ironing and I stayed on after I was married until my first baby was born so I worked there for eighteen years altogether.

We used to have to work very hard and sometimes we didn't used to get done until ten o'clock on a Friday evening. All the boyfriends used to stand outside waiting for the girls to come out. At the back of the laundry was a very steep hill, running down into Old London Road and they used to take the washing home on a cart, and one of the boys that worked there, he loaded the cart up and took it down over the back and upset all the washing down into the road.

When I was about fifteen years of age, my friend and me used to go

down to the Pier on a Sunday afternoon. We used to pay a shilling to go in and have our tea instead of going all the way home again. Sometimes we used to have salmon sandwiches which were quite a treat when we were young. My father used to pay for us to see the pantomime. We used to have to walk all the way down from Ore and all the way back home over the West Hill at night, but we used to enjoy the pantomime very much. We sat upstairs, which they used to call the gods.

The house I lived in as a child was a four roomed house, two up and two down and a scullery. My grandfather bought our house and my mother bought it from him. I had to sleep at my grandmother's because there were only two bedrooms and the boys used to sleep in one room and Mum and Dad had the other bedroom. We weren't allowed to stay up late at night. We had a tin bath and bathed in front of the fire and when we got older we used to go round the public baths. We cooked on a coal fire, with an oven at the side. We didn't have birthday parties or a cake, but we did have presents. We had a gramophone. My father had a whistle pipe. We had a magic lantern. We used to take it down in the cellar and show it there—we used to have other children in. They used to like to look at it.

Do you know I was only three at the time yet I can always remember my grandfather's funeral. There was a horse and carriage and we all went, all us children went. I remember Uncle Ernie's wedding. He was married at All Saints Church, they didn't have any bridesmaids or anything like that.

I don't think we went anywhere with our parents. We used to have outings at school. Always went to the school outings. To London, to the Zoo and St. Paul's Cathedral. We used to see the Houses of Parliament. We travelled by train. We went on Sunday school outings to Pevensy and Rye and Herstmonceaux Castle. I think we went by coach. First I went to Christ Church Sunday school, but they only used to go in a cart up to Fairlight for their outings. Once I was talking in Sunday school and they told me to go out, so we all left and went down to Halton.

My father didn't go to pubs and he didn't drink at all. He played football for St. Helen's. My uncle ran that. And two of my uncles played. My Uncle Tom only had one leg so he used to be linesman.

Rose with Fred Cornford

As a child I mostly played with the Whites and Bakers. We played hopscotch, hoops, that sort of thing. We did get dirty. My mother wasn't too strict about that sort of thing.

We had a dog and a cat and some bantams. We used to have the eggs for our breakfast from the bantams. Sometimes we used to go fishing with my dad. He used to go fishing all day over Fairlight Glen and sometimes he took us and we stayed all day and took sandwiches. We was discouraged from belonging to organisations like Scouts or Guides; my mother couldn't afford the uniforms. We had pocket money—sixpence—a week between four of us! And as one left school the others shared the sixpence. We spent it mostly on a halfpenny lucky bag—things like that. We used to sell jam jars. We used to get a halfpenny for a jam jar.

I remember my mother having a baby. I was about thirteen then, and that died. My grandfather died when we were young. And we had uncles and aunts. But we didn't have a lot to do with my father's relations. I don't think my parents had any special friends. No-one was invited to the house.

I think my parents paid insurance, but we never had any help from the Guardians, or the Parish, or any charity.

I first went to school when I was two and a half. My mother had another baby so she sent me to school early. And when I was thirteen they thought I was fourteen and I had to take my birth certificate to school. There was about forty in a class. They were quite big classes. Some teachers had to take two classes. I liked school and most of the teachers. Some were strict and one used to knock you round the head, knock your ears. Sometimes you were stood in the corner, or sometimes you just had the cane. After that I went to the Secondary School which had just started in Priory Road, but I didn't go there for very long. At eleven you sat an exam and if you were ever so good you went to the High School, but if you were't quite so good you went to the Secondary School, and if you didn't pass for those, you went to Ore Village or Clive Vale. In the Secondary School I went to, the classes weren't quite so big, but there was quite a few children in the class. We had French, English, arithmetic, writing. Most of the lessons that we had before. You could stop on there longer until you were sixteen but I had to leave at fourteen. I didn't want to stay on longer, because when you left school you earned money. You really didn't get much when you was at school.

TOM ROGERS

Born 1912

I was second youngest in the family, with nine brothers and sisters; five girls and four boys.

We all started at Ore Infant's School, where Ore Centre is now, and I remember my sisters taking me, when I was about five years old. Apart from that I can't remember much about it. I think we had about thirty in the class and I stayed there until I was eight years old, when we moved into the Old Town. And there I went to Clive Vale until I left school when I was fourteen years old.

I never did like school. It was all right, no problem, but I think most youngsters don't like school. I suppose it was no stricter than anywhere else; we had the usual punishments: the cane, lines after school and all that sort of thing. One thing they were pretty strict on was school attendance. If you didn't attend school the old school attendant was soon around your house to see what had happened and where you were. Otherwise I don't think it was any different to what it is today as far as discipline goes.

I've had the occasional caning at school; we were on the second floor up, you see, where the wash basins were. We used to make these paper bombs, fill them with water, and drop them on people as they went by. Got caught and, of course, got a caning for it.

I had two Headmasters; their name was Chambers, and they were two brothers. They were called Little Beak and Big Beak. I remember them well. And then we had Technical School which was down the bottom. We had a woodwork teacher name of Dermott, Dickie Dermott. On one particular time he went out of school and Jack Mitchell, that lives opposite us in Clifton Road, he got up on the bench and started doing the Charleston which was in fashion at that particular time. And the teacher caught him. They finished up having a fight on the floor these two, Jack Mitchell and the teacher. I don't know what happened after, but he got punished. This particular teacher, if you were doing something wrong, he had teeny bits of wood, sawn off from the pieces of wood, and he used to throw them at you. Or he'd have a piece of batten in his hand and he'd give you a belt across the knuckles with that.

I liked sport best, I suppose; football, cricket, swimming; swimming, mostly, in the sea or the swimming baths. I belonged to the Hastings and St Leonards Swimming Club later, when I was about seventeen or eighteen.

Until I was eight, or so, we lived in Ore. Dad had the pub there, the Oddfellows Arms, and we used to get a penny pocket money from one or two of the customers in the bar. One of them was a chap called One-Eye, One-Eyed Scrace, and every Saturday he used to give us kids a penny each. One of the old dustmen. I don't know why he was called One-Eye because as far as I know he had both perfectly good eyes.

He used to go eeling with my eldest brother Charlie. When the pub closed at night at ten o'clock they used to get their ricks and go right out in the country beating the waters for eels. They used to come home on Sunday mornings with their ricks full of eels. We used to have a big zinc bath in the yard that we'd sit these eels in and us kids used to play with them. Darned great big eels. And when the place was shut Dad used to clean them and cook them. They were lovely. Stewed eels.

When we was a young family, Dad and Mum used to take us right down over Fairlight Down into the Glen on Sunday afternoons and even very early in the morning. It was nice up through there then, lovely.

We very seldom saw Gran; we didn't like her at all. We occasionally used to go to tea with her, and if we did it was murder. You daren't put your elbows on the table or she'd have the toasting fork at you. Used to keep it on the table and poke your elbows. Very strict.

I used to go walking a lot, right over Fairlight, down over the Hog's Back and out on to a place called the Benches. Under Fairlight. Winkling, bring back a load of winkles. Dad used to cook them in a big steel boiler. Oh, they were lovely, they were. We had a garden at the pub, and us kids used to play in it. We had fruit trees and that to climb, and my brother Cecil made a big cave that went right back underneath the road. We used to have bottles of lemonade and all types of things in there. All the kids from Fairlight Road, Browns, Saxbys, Harmers and all those people, all used to play in there. There was a tall

Tom, on his father's knee, and family

Ore Village School

fence round the back of our garden, and we used to climb over the top and slide down the staves that used to run up against the fence. Well, one girl named Doris Harmer she slid down there one day, and she caught her britches on the staves and tore her britches open. Wasn't half in trouble when she got home.

Dad had his garden down the back of Victoria Avenue, running up to Old London Road. Grew his own pigs and all. Everyone had allotments. My mother made jams and pickles and things and she used to serve in the bar as well, you see. We used to have a woman come in and do our washing on a Monday and help out in the house, but Mother was nearly always in the bar.

Meals; well for breakfast, cereals weren't around then, mostly bread and jam; and Dad grew all sorts of things, loved his garden. Grew near enough all his vegetables. And poaching was really in then; rabbits, pheasants, anything like that. Dad used to go shooting with the local butcher and people like that. And Charlie, my oldest brother, he used to work for Jimmy Kemp which was right opposite the pub, where Gray's is now, and they always got their bit of meat and stuff. Oh, I think we had plenty of meat, and that. In the Old Town during the summer months, holiday time, we never wore boots or shoes. They were taken away. We used to run the streets and on the beach barefoot. Oh no, we just could't afford to wear shoes.

Photographs show us very smartly dressed, but that was for a special occasion. Family occasion, family photo. But normally you just wore normal working clothes, school clothes. No such things as school uniforms then because you couldn't afford them. Did have special clothes for Sundays if you went to Sunday school, under pressure. My two big sisters used to have to drag me to Sunday school, and to school. My parents never went to church, they were in business, never had the time.

I left Ore when the other boys were nearly out to work. It was a poor area really, but it was a darn sight poorer for us down in the Old Town. When we moved down to High Street the only one working was Cecil. He was on the Waterworks, in the baths, and he was the only wage that was coming in. In the whole family! Dad used to go down on the beach and help pull the boats up for a bit of fish for our meal. I used to play with various boys from the school, wherever I was. I didn't have any particular friends, I used to play with anybody. When we was in the Bourne I was about nine year old and I used to play with various kiddies in the street. Mostly fisher-folk. Or we used to play in the garden at the back of our place in the Bourne. We had a long garden. There was a big wall. It's still there now, and we used to play ball against that.

While I was at school I was already doing a part-time job. I started work when I was eleven years old and I worked for the baker next door, that was in the Bourne, delivering bread and that, a chap name of Wilson. I used to go and help him mix the dough, deliver bread, clean the fires out, sift all the ashes, that type of thing. That was on school days, and then on Saturdays I used to go all day and Sunday morning. He used to have a bike, a big baker's bike with a big carrier back and front to hold these big baskets, and I used to have to meet him up by Plynlimmon Road every Saturday with two big baskets of bread. He would take the bread and I used to go back and do odd jobs around the kitchen and that. I worked there for two or three years, and then I got a job in the hairdressers; old Bob Busby's up in High Street and I did about six years' apprenticeship altogether. He used to pay me about four shillings a week, and of course any tips I got were mine.

Course, as I say, Cecil and I were the only ones with money coming in at all. Sis was out of work, Florrie was out of work. Cecil was only getting seven shillings and sixpence a week as a tradesman, learning a trade. I used to go home every dinner time, run home, have my dinner, go round to the hairdressing salon, get half an hour in the shop lathering; and then I used to run all the way to school. Then when we left school at four o'clock I used to go straight home, have a bit of quick tea, and I'd be in the shop from about five o'clock until eight at night. And then, of course, weekends, I used to work all day Saturdays, and Sunday mornings. We was open from eight to twelve every Sunday morning.

One morning he said to me 'One of my customers has died up in Ockendens Passage, and there's a good chance for you to practise your shaving. They want him shaved before they lay him out'. So I took all the shaving gear with me, went up there, knocked on the old door and of course the old wife let me in, and I went upstairs. He was laid on a bed, one of the old-fashioned beds with the clip underneath to keep the springs in place. Well I lathered the old boy and I turned his face over to shave right down one side and I must have leaned against the bed, and it wasn't locked. I leaned, it pressed the mattress over and the thing just folded down into the metal frame. Course the old boy had got no bedclothes on to hold him there; he just sort of rolled over, dropped in between the bed and the floor and as he fell, all the wind in his body just got pumped out—poof! I tell you I shot down those stairs and out of the door and I never did go back for my kit. My governor just laughed his head off. I don't know if I was terrified or not. I wasn't very old, still at school.

Later on, we moved from the Old Town to Hollington. Dad was the caretaker of Hollington School, where he died, and Mum died at Hollington. When I worked for Henekey's wine stores I used to go to and fro from there.

I don't remember many Christmases when I was very young, but we used to have the normal Christmas parties and that when we was at home, but then of course Mum and Dad both died young so we didn't have many. There wasn't much money about then, Dad was only a caretaker.

While I was working at Bob Busby's there was a fish salesman used to come in each morning for a shave. His name was Ben Martin. Used to auction the fish. It was getting towards Christmas time and he came in and had this shave and he said to my governor 'Are you going to have one of my raffle tickets?'. My governor said 'Yeh, I'll have one, give the lad one as well', so he pulled out one of these tickets. I can always remember the name: 'Garnets Christmas Draw'. It was a smashing draw, and damned if I didn't go and win it. It was a London firm I think, anyway it was a super prize, a hamper from Selfridges: a turkey, a York ham, 50 cigars, 200 cigarettes, 12 bottles of wine, 12 bottles of whisky and a Christmas pudding. And that was the time when we didn't know where the next meal was coming from. Dad was out of work, could only go down the market and pick up a bit of fish. Of course, it was a godsend to us. There was also twenty five pounds cash. I gave the money to Mum. I had a bike out of it, we ate the food, and I gave my old governor a bottle of Scotch and the rest I gave to Dad. I fell off the bike coming down by Summerfields. Finished up on the grass, right off the pavement.

When I was about fourteen year old I left school and went into the hairdressing. I was glad to leave, I never cared for school. When I started hairdressing, still at school, I got four or five bob a week. When I left there I went up to Percy Ambler's up in Ore right next to the Oddfellows. They used to have a little sweet shop one side and on the other was the hairdressers. I worked there for about three years and then my sister said there was a vacancy down at Henneky's. I didn't even finish my apprenticeship. My dad wasn't half mad, but it was much more money, you see, and I worked there eleven years till I went into the Army. I did the cleaning, then served in the bar, cellar work, that kind of thing.

ALF HODD

Born 1922

My mother died when I was a little baby, and we were in with my Gran and my Grandfather. I started school right on my third birthday at the old Sandown School in School Road. It was boys and girls together in the same classroom, but not in the same playground. The majority of teachers were women, but the headmaster and two other teachers were men. They took the top junior classes. I should imagine that there would be thirty-five to forty in a class. But some teachers took two classes at the same time—one class sat at one end of the room, and the other class at the other end.

When I started I remember distinctly going in there. There was a big open fire with a guard right round it, and a big train, and a big dolls' house. The teacher sat me in the train and I didn't want to stay. My grandmother went home, and as soon as I thought she was indoors and the teacher wasn't looking I was out—home. Gran gave me a hiding and took me back, and the teachers said 'Oh, he'll be alright Mrs Hodd. You leave him'. As soon as my Gran got out of the door I remember the teacher giving me a hiding, and sitting me in the train, and saying 'Now stay there', which I did.

I remember we used to have a sleep in the afternoon, lying on little beds. I don't remember much about the lessons. All I remember really is the big blackboard. We went through the infants. There was Miss Phillips, Miss Compton and Miss Stratton. But really it was Mrs Stratton I suppose, because they had a farm at North Seat. My Gran used to take us up there if it was a nice Sunday afternoon, and have a cup of tea and a cake in her garden. She had a big goldfish pond. I know her son ran the farm, so although we called her Miss Stratton it must have been Mrs Stratton. The term Mrs was never used. Then we went into Miss Moores. The next one was a man, Mr Vincent. Then the next class was Miss Hornbrook, but Mr Divall, the headmaster, he took music for those classes with his little tuning fork. The top class was Mr Matthews who took the two classes. We stayed there until we were eleven.

We used to like football, but very few had a pair of proper football boots, but that didn't matter. We used to play on the East Hill and on the Glebe along Halton. It wasn't cissy like it is now with no contact. You could contact then alright. I played football in a pair of gymshoes, and I must have broken my toe and split the bone because a swelling came on top and started forming a separate part. I didn't say anything until I started walking a bit like a cripple, and my Gran spotted it.

So I went over to St Helens Hospital and had it trimmed off. They chloroformed me and I came round sick. All the kids had their tonsils out. All the beds were up on blocks of wood, and every kid was being sick. As soon as he smelt the ether or anything he was sick again for a couple of days. That was the children's ward at St Helens. At the end of the children's ward was the infants' ward, for babies. I had to go along and hold the bottles for the babies to feed them. I always remember Mrs Streeter coming in and feeding the children—wet nursing them—which I thought was funny at the time. It was very nice, but it was more like being in the army. It was all discipline. There was no doing as you like, like there is now. Two visitors was two visitors. The sister didn't seem to be just in charge of the ward, she absolutely owned it.

For infectious diseases they went to Mount Pleasant Hospital. It was the sanatorium, and it was the isolation hospital for the whole of Hastings. I remember vividly vaccinations. We all went over to St Helens Hospital and queued up. They'd vaccinate a dozen and then a couple would faint. As soon as you got your vaccination your mother put a little bit of red ribbon, so you all went back to school with a little bit of red ribbon tied round the armpit you were vaccinated on.

We started school at nine o'clock. A bell used to ring, and we used to line up in the playground. The majority of the kids came from Sandown; Percy Road, Clifton Road, Church Street, and that area. We had breakfast at home, but on most mornings my mother had to go to St Helens Hospital for her treatment. In that case, or if she felt ill and didn't get up very early, she would bring it over and we would go out of class and have it in the porch. Not every morning, but a good many mornings. That would be half past nine or a quarter to ten, before the morning break. At eleven o'clock, if she was home, she would bring us across a piece of cake and a cup of milk. If she didn't, you looked down at all the mothers standing in School Road passing it through to see who got the best cake, then you'd go and stand by them and say 'Hello Mrs Edwards', or who ever, and they'd say 'Hello Alfie' and break the cake in half and give you half. Of course if you was quick you'd be quick enough to get up to another mother, if one was coming a bit late.

The dinner break was from twelve to half past one, but as we got into the juniors everybody had school dinners then, which was in the basement of a house that I think was next to the church at the top of Clifton Road. It was cooked there, and you had the forms and the trestles. You had wonderful soups and duffs. Then after a time it was moved to over Feists, the bakers, opposite the Oddfellows. It was more like a party up there. They did nice dinners there. We always had school dinners—free—of course.

The juniors finished at four o'clock, but the infants came out at half past three. You usually had a cooked meal at night It was nearly always rabbit stew or roast rabbit. I can smell it now. Rabbit, rabbit, rabbit. By the 1930's there was no soup kitchen in Ore that I knew of. The soup kitchens were earlier. There was one in Sandown Chapel, but I couldn't remember that.

The third class in the infants they taught us raffia and cane work and basket work, because I suppose they thought well, that is all the majority of you will be any good for when you leave school. But I don't know that anybody ever touched it after they left school.

Our teachers were very strict. With hindsight you can see why, because if a kid got half a chance to get out of step he was there. And once it had happened, if the teacher didn't give him a hiding, he'd have no authority in the class at all. The teachers were there all the time. You never had a new teacher. All the parents knew the teachers, and the teachers knew every parent. The parents thought the teacher was something. Teaching was a profession. In those days it must have been vocational. They had student teachers. Some teachers had degrees, some didn't have degrees, but they could get a forty class and manage everyone in that class. At the junior school, if one of those teachers walked past any parent in that area they would always pass the time of day. They would never walk pass the teacher. They would always acknowledge the teachers, men and women.

I remember two teachers at Clive Vale School, Big Beak and Little Beak they called them. You could never find out just by talking to kiddies what those two teachers real names were. Father and son, I think they were. But they were called Big Beak and Little Beak, and never called anything else.

I went over Sandown School one dinnertime. I was coming up eleven. Up the pipe, on to the roof. I think I got four tennis balls out the valleys in the roof. The deputy headmaster, he said, 'You was on the roof, you've got some balls'. I said 'Yes'. He said 'Where are they?'. I said 'I took them home'. He said 'Well, you stole them then'. I said 'No, because if I hadn't have taken them they'd have laid up there for ever, and just rotted away'. He said, 'Well, I say you stole them'. So I went home and told my Gran, and my Gran came over there and there was a hell of a row. But they didn't get the balls back. And then my sister was in another class. Although she was older than me, she was in a lower class. I think the teacher gave her a clip round the ear for something, and she told my Gran. So my Gran went over. We heard this commotion in my classroom. My teacher, a man teacher, nipped out into the porch to see what was happening, and my Gran was clipping the teacher's ear. But they were only very isolated cases.

My father and his brothers all went to Sandown School. My Grandmother never went to school. She used to pay tuppence a week, or something like that, to learn to read and write. But Grandfather, he couldn't read or write.

All the games we played at school were all out of door. Football. Not much cricket went on. In those days we played football all the year round. But there didn't seem to be much football in the streets, probably because all around there was steep hills. But our own games after school, although some of them were mischievous, there was no vandalising. When the gas man came round putting the street lights on with a pole with a hook on the end, he'd pull the chain and light the lamp, then you would wait for him to get down the bottom of the road, and just before he disappeared into the valley between School Road and Church Street we would shin up the post, and pull the other chain and put it out. As he went down into the valley he would look back, and see the lamp was out. He would scratch his head. He couldn't see anyone, and he'd come back and put it on.

There were marbles, cigarette cards or fag cards, hoops, tops; they were the main ones. They seemed to start on the same day every year, so someone must have known something. Conkers—we knew what time of the year they were. Conkers was quite an art, because different boys had different ways of making the horse chestnuts hard. Some used to soak them in salt water, some in vinegar, some used to bake them.

That wasn't a game, it was taken seriously. When two were playing conkers everybody was standing round watching to see that it was all above board. Of course if a kiddie said he had a twenty-er or a thirty-er, which meant that he'd smashed twenty of thirty other conkers, you wanted to know whether it was true or not. If one had got a good conker, you knew he had a good conker, because you could see what he'd been doing with it.

The two main games in the road were barbery double and tip cat. Tip cat was a six inch stick, about half inch by five-eighths across, pointed at both ends. Tacked onto the end was a longer stick, and when it went up into the air you had to see how far you could hit it.

Barbery double was a sort of hide and seek game, with one showing himself now and then and one trying to catch, but normally the one who started the game, the catcher, he packed up and went home before the game finished. If he couldn't have a turn jumping out and hiding he wouldn't want to play. You had the old milk tin with two or three stones in it, then you squashed the top in and stand it in a circle in the middle of the road, and then you had to run and kick it as far as you could, and the other one had to run and pick it up, and when he went to pick it up you would run. He had to rattle the can when he came after you, so you knew where he was and he didn't know where you were. With barbery double you could go miles. It was not much good working out to the country, it was too open. But from Sandown you could go along Oakfield Road, up Frederick Road, up the High Bank and down. You didn't have to stop there if it was a good game and a good crowd. Most games were played along Oakfield Road. That was called the brickyard then, because the houses on the hospital side weren't built—that was allotments and a slaughter house. The other side was the row of houses, and the waste ground along the end where the brick works used to be. That road wasn't made up. It was a rough road. If you was playing in Sandown, somebody would come out and shout out, 'Why don't you go and play round the brickyard?'. These games went on well after dark, until you'd hear somebody calling 'Come on Tommy, come on Gerry, come on Billy'. They were games played by gangs of boys. Most girls had to be in before dark.

If you went to the Salvation Army six weeks before the summer outing and got six stars in your book you were eligible to go. The same with the Christmas party. Sandown Sunday school was the same. These outings, we went to Wadhurst, Battle, Fairlight and sometimes in the summer, if it was a party, we went on the vicarage lawn. As far as we were concerned going to Battle was as good as going to Margate. You had no need to go to Battle for anything on the transport, and it was too far to walk, so it was somewhere to go. When the outing was over the teachers used to go to your house and say you weren't there, and the parents would say 'I'll see that he is next Sunday'. You went once then you stopped.

On Saturday afternoons we had the Band of Hope where they gave you a bag of sweets to go. The man was standing there with a stick which he tapped the floor with for the next magic lantern slide. But then you'd bang the floor while he was telling you about the slide, and it would go along, and the lecturer would say 'Put it back'. We all had these bags of sweets, and in one of the bags was a piece of paper, and if you got that bit of paper you got a coconut bar. That was the lucky bag. We thought that was fiddled quite a few times by the women teachers. I never got one myself. On Mother's Day they'd give you a flower to take home.

Part Two
Hastings Schools and Education
1800–1945

HASTINGS SCHOOLS AND EDUCATION

1800–1945

Exploring the history of schools and education in Hastings is a difficult and uphill struggle. Information is often scrappy and incomplete, particularly for schools in the nineteenth century teaching the poorest children. As the Hastings school directory illustrates (part three of this book) some schools moved from place to place, sometimes changing their names, while on other occasions disappearing altogether, perhaps re-emerging elsewhere at a later date. In other cases the same sites, and often the same buildings, were used by a number of different schools.

Rather than duplicate existing work on schools in Hastings, particularly the number of accounts of individual schools[1], the aim is to sketch the overall picture—the number and type of schools, the shape of education in the town, and some of the most important issues and arguments at particular times.[2]

Ragged, British and National Schools

In the early nineteenth century education in Hastings appears to have been largely provided by three different types of school—endowed or charity schools, dame schools, and church schools. In general the system of education was unplanned and inadequate on a number of counts, and sometimes grossly mis-managed. Unlike today, neither central nor local government played much of a role in education in the town in the first decades of the century.

However, quite early on in the nineteenth century Parliament and central government became concerned about education nationally. Slowly at first, and then at a quickening pace toward the end of the century, it began to intervene in the finance and organisation of education, increasingly determining the type of schools, what was taught, and so on. These changes were felt in Hastings in a number of ways.

Perhaps the first local evidence of the beginnings of national concern was a Parliamentary survey of education in Hastings in 1818.[3] The survey reported that there were nineteen schools in Hastings and one in 'Oare'. There were none in St Leonards, which was still a decade away from its development as a new town by Burton.

Of the nineteen schools in Hastings thirteen were 'day schools' taught by mistresses 'in which 300 are instructed'—an average of twenty-three children per school. There was a further day school 'taught by a master, containing 13 children'. These fourteen schools are probably best thought of as dame schools. No further information is known to exist about them, although dame schools nationally were often inadequate, simply springing up to meet local demands without any regulation or checking of standards. The lowliest kind were where women looked after children, perhaps teaching them to read, knit and sew, for whatever parents could afford.

Of somewhat more importance, in terms of the number of children involved, were the three church schools in Hastings. Two of these were Sunday schools, 'one belonging to Dissenters, in which 150 children are instructed, and the other 120'. The third church school was a combined day and Sunday school attended by 100 children. The school in Ore, 'for boys and girls, in which 66 scholars are taught, supported by the rector', was also clearly a church school.

Ore at the time appears to be a good instance of one of the major problems in early nineteenth century education—opposition by employers and many of the most powerful on the grounds that schooling would reduce their workforce and lead to revolutionary ideas. The authors of the 1818 survey note that: 'The rector's school affords sufficient means of education for the poor, and they are in general desirious of having their children instructed; but this desire is not greatly encouraged by the farmers, who form a leading feature in the parish.'

Evidence of perhaps the first Sunday school in Hastings exists for 1800, when Edward Milward, a major landowner in the area (and clearly not an Ore farmer) records the payment of a guinea on August 31st, 'gave Sunday School'. By 1831 over 11,000 children had been admitted.[4] As the nineteenth century wore on the church, both established and nonconformist (the 'Dissenters' of the 1818 survey) became ever more important in education both nationally and locally.

The 1818 survey also provides evidence of the third type of school in

Hastings—three endowments meant for the support of charity or endowed schools in the town. All three appear to have been in a sorry state. One bequest was from John Ellsworth, in the form of the income from ninety-four acres of land that formed part of Priory farm. However, 'this never having been applied to the purposes intended for, the matter is now before the court of chancery'.

The two other endowments formed Parker's and Saunders' schools. Parker's charity school was for the 'education of poor children' in the town. Similarly, Saunder's endowment was for the education of 40 boys, 'to teach 20 poor girls to read and work' and for 'apprenticing 2 poor boys'. But both endowments according to Webster Whistler, rector, 'have been much mismanaged and underlet'. Only Parker's school was in operation, with 85 pupils. The major problem appears to have been dishonesty on the part of the mayor and corporation of Hastings who were charged with running the charities. Land—the prime asset of both charities—was let at far below market rates. In one case the mayor himself rented land from the charity for twenty pounds a year, while its annual value was in fact 166 pounds.

Half a century later, by the late 1860s, the education system of Hastings had changed in a number of ways. Dame schools seem to have all but disappeared from the town (although Saunders' Schools, were said to include two dame schools in 1868[5]). Provision by churches had expanded dramatically. Sunday schools, initially the major form of church involvement in schooling, had been supplemented and supplanted by church-run day schools. For the church, religious education was all important. Teaching children to read was not simply an end in itself, but as much a means of ensuring they could read the Bible. For much of the nineteenth century the Church of England and nonconformists were in an uneasy truce and sometimes open battle against each other as to who should win the hearts, minds and faith of children and parents. This struggle, which took place all over England, was much in evidence in Hastings itself.

Church of England schools were usually part of the 'National Society for promoting the education of the poor in the principles of the established church' (formed in 1811). 'National Schools' taught the liturgy and catechism of the Church of England. In contrast 'British Schools'—part of the 'British and Foreign School Society' founded in 1814—were run by nonconformists.

One instance of the struggle between the nonconformists and the established church occurred in the early 1870s in the London Road area of St Leonards. A British School had been established there for some years, while the rival Christ Church school was in most inadequate rented accommodation. The Rev. C.L. Vaughan of Christ Church launched an appeal to erect a new school building: 'In order to carry on a lasting mission work amongst the poor, new schools are a little short of an absolute necessity .... The only available school at present ... is struggling on to win souls to the love of Jesus and through the little ones to reach the hearts of parents. But it is wholly unequal to the task.' Vaughan totally ignored the existing British school. This drew a storm of protest from the nonconformists. The protesters were supported by the editor of the Hastings and St Leonards News: 'The plain fact is that the clergy of Christ Church assume that no teaching can be religious unless it is after their own type .... No man of candour, who really understands the case, can sanction an appeal which is really grounded on the assumption that no true religion is taught outside of Christ Church'.[6]

A survey by Hastings council in 1870[7] suggests that the following were Church of England Schools: Halton, St Clements and All Saints, St Mary's, St Mary Magdalen, St Leonards, St Paul's, and Holy Trinity. Most of these schools also had infant departments. Another infant school was associated with Christ Church church. British Schools existed for boys and girls in both Hastings and St Leonards. Other schools recorded in the survey were Parker's, a Saunder's School for boys and another for girls, a 'ragged' school in Tackleway, and Cavendish Place Infant School. The twenty-three schools in the survey had 1715 boys and 1663 girls on their rolls. The smallest was Saunder's Girls' with only twenty-two pupils, while the largest, St Mary's Parochial, had 373 children.

By 1870 Cavendish Place School was one of the longest established schools in Hastings, as well as being one of the most unusual, at least in its origins. It was founded in 1829, as part of the 'Infant School Society' for children between the ages of two and six. The society was a forward-looking national movement stressing moral and intellectual character, and making much use of toys, music and kindness in the classroom.

A ragged school existed in the Old Town at least from 1855, and another in Ore in 1871 and perhaps earlier. Ragged schools, some of which were part of the 'Ragged School Union' formed in 1844,

Halton School

St Paul's School

117

provided education for the very poorest and most deprived children, such as those excluded from other schools because of their poverty and character (Ore and the Old Town were the two poorest areas of Hastings).

Parker's and Saunders' endowed schools had survived the period between 1818 and 1870. But both received some damning criticism from a Mr Giffard reporting to the School Inquiry Commission of 1868.[8] Discipline in Parker's school was described as follows: 'The discipline is defective. The boys copy from each other without check or scruple, and are manifestly unaccustomed to a strict examination.' Giffard concluded: 'This school like many others of its type, has been allowed to sink to a level of a second-rate National school. Its downward course has been certain but gradual …. I do not think the school, under its present regime answers the intention of its founder or any other useful end.'

Saunders' schools fared a little better under Giffard's examination, but a number of criticisms were made. 'Latin is not taught in the school, "the parents and friends" of the boys being indifferent or

Hastings Grammar School

adverse to such instruction.' Saunders' dame schools were in rooms 'as confined and ill-ventilated as can be conceived'.

More important was Giffard's argument that both Parker's and Saunders' schools should charge 'moderate capitation fees with a view to improving the schools'. In his view poorer children were 'already abundantly provided for in a better way elsewhere', and the two charity schools should concentrate on the 'establishment of a good middle-class education'. As we have seen, however, in their origins both schools were aimed at poor children. the two foundations and schools did follow the course laid out by Giffard. They merged in 1878 to become the Hastings Grammar School and increasingly catered for middle-class children, despite their origins as charity schools for the poor. From this date until well into the second half of the twentieth century the new school functioned as the major boys' 'secondary' school in the town, access being based on rigorous selection, and to some extent at least ability to pay.

By May 1871[9] a further council survey gave somewhat different figures from the one a few months earlier. Twenty-eight 'elementary' schools are mentioned (including two being built). The schools were classified in a number of ways: twenty-five were public and three private; nineteen connected with the established church and nine 'conducted on unsectarian principles'; there were eight boys' schools, seven girls' schools, five mixed schools and eight infants schools; seventeen received annual grants from the Government and eighteen of the principal teachers were 'certificated'. Of the 3353 children on the roll, on average 2512 attended in 1870.

The schools catered for pupils between the ages of under three to twenty one and charged fees ranging from one penny to nine pence per week. Seventeen different subjects were offered: Reading (taken by 3,354 pupils), Writing (3,252), Arithmetic (2,967), Dictation (1,816), Religious Instruction (3,277), History (314), Grammar (499), Geography (936), Needlework (1,270), Kinder Garter (sic) work, Object Lessons etc (259), Drawing (11), Euclid (5), Navigation (1), French (11).

The 1871 survey shows that during the five decades to 1870 many new schools had been opened by both the established and nonconformist church. The educational map of the town had been redrawn. Often this was carried out with missionary fervour as at Halton. To quote a report on the building of a new infant school in 1859: 'The district attached to this incumbency is to a very great extent inhabited by a class of individuals among whom the restraints required by religion or imparted in education are needed to the fullest extent that their benign influence can reach. If such may be said of the parents, the same remark applies to the children ...'[10]. Much the same sentiments appeared on the foundation stone of St Mary Magdalen Schools, laid in December 1855: 'To promote the glory of God, by educating the children of the poor, according to His word, and in the doctrines and discipline of the Church of England.'[11]

But all was not well with education either nationally or locally. The problems of the endowed schools have already been discussed. Despite the existence of ragged schools, many of the poorest children did not attend school. Finance depended on voluntary contributions, and education was generally grossly under-funded (although British and National schools both received Government grants toward the cost of school building). Ratepayers often opposed the idea of paying for schools through the rates, particularly in the case of religious denominations other than their own. Many parents could not afford even one penny a week in fees, and some had no particular wish to see their children educated (especially if it meant that children could not earn often much needed money). Methods of teaching usually left much to be desired, with older children often teaching the younger ones. Some people in authority had no real belief in the value of education, indeed some argued against the 'over-education of the poor', and the 'subversive' nature of some schools.

The Government became increasingly concerned about the state of education in many places throughout Britain. While many individuals thought the church was doing a good job, increasingly it was accepted that other approaches were needed. After many years of national debate the result was the Elementary Education Act of 1870, 'the most workable piece of compromise legislation in English nineteenth-century history'.[12] This Act was to change the shape of education in Hastings.

The School Board

The 1870 Act left denominational schools untouched in areas where they were thought to work well and met local needs—typically these were places where the Church of England was strong. Elsewhere locally elected school boards were given powers to levy rates, build

PARISH OF ORE

ELECTION

OF

SCHOOL BOARD

I, the undersigned, being the Returning Officer for the Election of the School Board, held on the Twenty-second day of January, 1881, for the above-named parish, Do Hereby Give Notice that the under-mentioned persons have been duly Elected as Members of the School Board :---

Surnames.	Christian Names.	Places of Abode.	Descriptions.
DENNETT	Thomas ...	Ore	Ironmonger
DOUDNEY	David Alfred	The Rectory, Ore	Rector of Ore
GIBSON ...	John Thomas Stone	London road, Ore	Shoemaker
SPALDING	Thomas ...	Ore Place	Gentleman
THORPE....	George Archibald ...	High Croft, Ore	Gentleman

Given under my hand this Twenty-second day of January, 1881.

(*Signed*)

ARTHUR R. INSKIPP,

F. J. PARSONS, Printer, " Observer " Office, H-------

schools, provide teachers and if they thought fit, insist upon the attendance of all children who were not being educated in any other way. It was limited to children under thirteen; parents who could not afford payment were excused fees. As a result of the Forster Act, as it was known, a school board was formed for Hastings and St Leonards in 1871. It consisted of nine members; this number was increased to eleven in 1895. Two years later, on the extension of the borough boundaries, it assumed responsibility for board education in the parishes of Ore and Hollington.

The Act supplemented rather than replaced the existing church dominated system of education in Hastings. The schools run by the Church of England retained a largely independent status as 'voluntary' schools, although their work was increasingly guided and controlled by central Government.

In its turn, and particularly in its early years, the local board was dominated by the church, both established and nonconformist. On the founding of the Hastings board the two sides formed an uneasy alliance. They agreed a panel of candidates (the established church having one more than the nonconformists) to put before the electorate of ratepayers.

It is difficult to judge the extent the two groups agreed a common platform and programme of action for the board. Certainly their underlying beliefs were often fundamentally opposed, and there is evidence that at times serious differences surfaced. Early on in the existence of the board some representatives of the Church of England thought the best course would be to continue with the existing voluntary effort, hence restricting the activities of the Hastings board. The local press reported the board's meeting of June 7 1871, at which the Rev. Tottenham said 'seeing the flourishing state of education in the borough, that no schools would be required; he would at the next meeting move that an effort should be made by voluntary means to supply what was needed, without taxing the ratepayers. He himself would be very glad to give twenty-five pounds for such a purpose'.[13]

The ratepayer lobby to which Tottenham was appealing remained a major force throughout the thirty year existence of the school board, and continued into the running of education by Hastings council itself. In 1889-91 the average rate levied by the Hastings board was 2.66 pence, the lowest in Sussex and less than half the English borough average of 6.3 pence.

Tower Road School

Hastings United District School Board.

RULES for SCHOOL MANAGEMENT.

1. ADMISSION.---Children when they first come to any of the Schools should be brought by the Parent, or some person able to answer all necessary enquiries.

2. ATTENDANCE.---Parents are required to send their Children regularly, as the missing of lessons not only interferes with their progress, but is unjust to the Teachers, and seriously affects the results of the Examinations.

3. PAYMENTS.---The School Fees should be paid in advance each Monday Morning. Parents unable to pay must apply to the Board for remission.

4. NON-SCHOOL HOURS.---The Teachers do not in any case undertake the care of the Children in the dinner hour; but, in case of bad weather, those living at great distances may remain.

5. PUNCTUALITY and CLEANLINESS.---Children are required to be in their places when the School opens, both Morning and Afternoon. Parents are urged to send them clean.

6. INFECTIOUS DISEASES.---Parents are requested to take every precaution to prevent the spread of infectious diseases by keeping Children so afflicted from School, and by reporting the case to the Teacher.

7. WITHDRAWALS.---The Parents of Children leaving School are requested to give notice of such removal. It is of great importance that the Children should on no account absent themselves from the Examinations by Her Majesty's Inspector, of which due notice will be given.

Another issue raised at the same meeting by the representatives of the established church was 'where they were to send the rougher class of children to'. It was thought new schools such as St Pauls' might not care to have rough boys and, according to the Rev. Porter, the Ragged School might be the best option. In general the nonconformist members of the board were far more progressive than their established church colleagues, urging that the board be as active as possible. The local situation to some extent reflected the national scene— nonconformists were a major radical force for change at the time in education and other fields. In Hastings they were happy to see the local British schools transferred to the board. Most if not all of the National Schools stayed in the voluntary sector.

At times the truce between established church and nonconformists fell apart and the fundamental differences between the two were plain to see. In 1901 a furious argument raged over whether an unorthodox national anthem used to conclude the opening ceremony of the new St Helen's Mixed and Infant School was appropriate. The first line went 'God bless our native land', and not the established 'God save the Queen'.[14]

None the less, the sharing of control of the board between representatives of the established and nonconformist church was not disrupted until the later election of 'independent' candidates, including the Liberal Mrs Strickland (who by the early years of the next century was heavily involved in the suffrage movement locally).

Despite the Rev. Tottenham's wishes, the Hastings board was very active. Two schools—Hollington and Waterloo Place—seem to have been opened as board schools within two years of the passing of the Forster Act. Some schools which were already in existence—Ore Village School and the two British Schools in Hastings and St Leonards—became board schools. By the end of the century further board schools had been built: Clive Vale, Manor Road, Silverhill, Sandown, Priory Road, Mount Pleasant, Tower Road, and West St Leonards. In general the Hastings board acted to provide new schools in those neighbourhoods the church was unable or unwilling to operate in as an educational provider.

The new board schools were typically very substantial and well built Victorian buildings. A typical layout was a central hall surrounded by six or more classrooms. Single sex schools were more usual than mixed sex schools, and where the latter were built entrances and playgrounds, although not classrooms, were usually separate. It was in these buildings that thousands of Hastings children were educated in later decades. Many of them survive today, often retaining their educational use. The Hastings school board was typical of boards throughout Britain in providing what was known as 'elementary' education to the age of thirteen for ordinary working class children—middle class children attending local secondary schools such as Hastings Grammar School.

By the end of 1900 there were places for 6186 children in board schools and 5202 in voluntary schools.[15] In thirty years, and mostly through new building, Hastings school board had easily passed the provision made by the voluntary sector.

One of the major problems faced by the board in Hastings (and, indeed, all over Britain) was simply that of ensuring children attended school. For example, average attendance for 1890 was 76.5 per cent. On any day little more than three out of four children were likely to be present. There were a number of reasons for low attendance.[16] Before 1870, and in some places 1880, children were not compelled, by law, to attend school. The idea was new and many children and parents resisted compulsion. Other reasons for absence included obvious causes such as illness (schools, particularly infant schools, were sometimes closed through epidemics of contagious diseases such as scarlet fever, whooping cough and even smallpox). Some children stayed away simply because they did not want to go to school, perhaps rebelling against the often strict diet of drill and discipline. In other cases they were absent to look after sick members of the family or to work. Many teachers and members of the board thought parental attitudes, behaviour and discipline had a lot to do with the matter. Certainly some parents gave their children little or no support at school, and others put their children under considerable pressure to truant and work. Some periods of the year were notable for the extent of absences. In late September and early October most of Ore seems to have been away hop picking. In many situations poor attendance was related to poverty. When in 1891 the board stopped charging school fees to any parents—the first free school system in Hastings—attendance improved—to 83.3 per cent in 1899.

The board had a number of sanctions against absence. The first step was a visit by the 'Attendance Officer', usually known (even long after school boards had disappeared) as the 'school board man'. The visit

Silverhill School

usually occurred the day following an absence. An attendance 'Notice' would be issued, and if this had no effect parents would be taken before the Magistrates. This happened in 390 cases between 1898 and 1900, and as a result 192 'Attendance Orders' were issued, 144 people fined, twenty-three cases dismissed or withdrawn, and thirty-one children sent to Industrial School or Truant School. Truant School—the one at Purley Lodge (Brighton) was often used—was the ultimate sanction. The problem of school attendance persisted throughout the first half of the twentieth century.

Another problem in some schools was that of discipline. In most cases it was enforced in a number of ways—the layout of the classroom, the use of drill, physical punishments (particularly using the cane) and so on—and never got out of hand. But some schools were particularly difficult, with teachers being subject to physical violence from pupils and parents. The logbook for Sandown Mixed School is revealing. In 1894 a pupil raised a poker to the teacher. On 18th July 1895 the log reords: 'Charles Cornford kicked, fought, and punched Miss Ashbee and for this he was severley punished. He swore at her. The mother came up with many more and caused a great disturbance. She also swore. A policeman was sent for and he came and escorted all the teachers safely away from the school where they had been locked in for 2 hours and five minutes.'

A number of boys from the school were sent to Purley Truant

School, another (in 1897) to a reformatory for three years, and in March 1898 a boy was sent to Lewes Goal for seven days. Not all teachers survived the experience of Sandown School for long. In June 1897 one new teacher lasted the morning, declining the job because the children 'are of too rough a character'.[17]

By the turn of the century the control by the church of the board was weaker than in the 1870s. Independents had been elected to the board, and had made their voices heard. In June 1900 the board decided to abolish the annual examinations in 'Scripture knowledge'. Even so religious instruction in Hastings board schools still included a morning service 'opened by singing a hymn followed by a short prayer, and a period of thirty minutes devoted to reading portions of Scripture in accordance with the Syllabus'.[18]

Hastings Council and Education

In the late 1890s there was increasing national debate about the future of the school boards.[19] With hindsight they can be seen as part of a transition from a private and church dominated system to one controlled by central and local government.

School boards, including the one for Hastings, were swept away with the Education Act 1902. They were replaced by new local education committees which ran education on behalf of local authorities. For the first time Hastings Corporation was the most important educational provider in the town. It also had the task 'of promoting the general co-ordination of all forms of education'. Voluntary schools were taken under the wing of the council which, for example, paid the teachers. The managers of these 'non-provided' schools, as they became known, did, however, provide the school building free of charge to the education authority for use as a elementary school.

This arrangement brought a storm of opposition in Hastings and elsewhere from nonconformists, and Labour and Liberal parties. They protested at being compelled to pay, through the rates, for the teaching of Anglicanism. At one local protest meeting, held in the Concert Hall, St Leonards in April 1904, the Rev. Wenyon described the problem as 'the compelling of Nonconformists to provide the funds for a propaganda aimed at the destruction of Nonconformity'.[20] This fight

Ore Village Boys' School with Mr Whitfield, headmaster of 25 years in May 1910

was one of the factors that contributed to the return to power of the reforming Liberal government in the general election of 1906 (Hastings was one of only two constituencies in the country to have a Tory gain).

The change from board to council had relatively little impact on local elementary education. Some former school board members, such as Mrs Strickland, who were also councillors became members of the education committee. Many of the same people remained as managers of individual schools. What was taught was slow to change. Religious instruction was as before. Discipline, patriotism and respect for the status quo figured large. It was quite in order for the Conservative MP for Hastings, Arthur du Cros, to provide all children with a Christmas tea in their classrooms. Open days, Empire Day and the like all contained a good deal of flag waving and, in the performance of 'action songs', fun was often poked at groups such as the suffragettes.

The council still had the same problems—such as that of attendance—to deal with. Committee members visited the Truant School in Brighton. Most were pleased with what they saw, although E.H. Jukes, chairman of the school attendance sub-committee, reported 'I was impressed with the fear that the life at the school may leave a feeling of degradation on the minds of the boys that may be difficult to efface. It is too much of the prison life and standard. Brighton, with twice the population of Hastings, sends but one boy to its own school, and, I understand, to stop truanting, persistently fines the parent'.[21] Despite the comment, use was still made of the school.

Hastings council did introduce bye-laws on the employment of children, which included clauses such as 'No child who is liable to attend school shall be employed in or about any barber's shop ... or in or about any licensed public house, or in or about any premises licensed for public entertainment'.[22] The evidence from part one of this book is that many employers flouted the law.

One perhaps surprising change on the issue of attendance is that in 1906 the education committee agreed to stop awarding medals for regular attendance at school. This action was on the recommendation of Hastings Head Teachers Association and the Medical Officer of Health. The former argued that the use of medals was 'productive of harm rather than good', that sick and infectious children sometimes still went to school to qualify for medals, and that it was unjust to sick children forced to stay at home.[23]

Board of Education inspectors usually provided good reports on the

'Kitchener's Army' as portrayed by Halton School infants, March 1915

'Examples of the shrieking sisterhood portrayed to the life'. A prize day 'tableaux' of suffragettes by children of Clive Vale School, April 1910

Halton Girls' School—'Britannia's Flag', December 1910

teaching in Hastings schools. For Priory Road School in 1903, for example, the inspector reported that the boys' school was 'An admirably conducted School'; that 'The girls' department continues in a high state of efficiency, both as regards discipline and attainments'; and that 'The infants are under excellent influence, and the discipline and instruction deserve high commendation'.

Most criticism was reserved for the school buildings. An inspector reported that for Cavendish Place (one of the oldest school buildings in the town) 'Additional Cloakroom accommodation is needed, and one end of the mainroom is dark. The playground in its present condition is useless except in the finest weather. The babies' room, which is awkwardly shaped and inconveniently small, forms the only entrance to the teacher's house'. Some schools—such as Halton, Ore Village and Sandown—were described as 'difficult'. This seems to have meant that the inspector thought they were in rough neighbourhoods and that discipline was likely to be a problem.[23]

Not everyone in Hastings agreed with the work of the education committee. In June 1903 thirty-eight 'Ratepayers' wrote objecting to the fact that the management board of Hollington School 'contains no representative of the Working-classes, who are 85 per cent. of the inhabitants of the district', and no parents or (with one exception) local people.[25] More typical lobbying came from ratepayers complaining about the 'excessive cost of Education in this town'.[26] In response to this pressure the education committee appointed a special sub-committee 'to consider and report whether, and if so how, any reduction can be made in the expenditure on Elementary and Higher Education in the Borough'. The result was a reduction in the number of teachers employed.[27]

The council's new education responsibilities came just at the time that Hastings was entering a period of several decades of economic stagnation. The population of the town actually fell between 1901 and 1911, and did not show many signs of recovery until after the Second War. This had a huge impact on the work of the education committee. Whereas the school board had opened many new schools and, in the 1890s, had confidently looked forward to further future expansion, the council had the opposite situation to contend with. For example, by 1917 there was accommodation in Hastings elementary schools for 9,967 children. Average attendance, however, was only 59.7 per cent— four out of ten places were not taken. Throughout the first half of the twentieth century little new school building went on in Hastings.

Balfour's 1902 Act also gave education authorities the power to provide not only elementary schools but also secondary education after the age of thirteen. Following the Act, and right up until 1945, Hastings council explored and in some cases tried a range of different schemes for secondary education in the town. For a long period, however, the council was in something of a cleft stick. On one hand some councillors could see the need for secondary education, and the borough was being encouraged to provide it by the Board of Education in London. On the other hand the ratepayer lobby was very powerful, and many existing school building were under-used. The result was often inappropriate and inadequately funded schemes.

Early on the question of boys' secondary education did not detain the council for long. The vast majority of children were expected to leave school at thirteen (some even going half-time at the age of ten). The few to enter secondary education either paid fees (too expensive for most families) or competed for scholarships to Hastings Grammar School. The question of girls' secondary education was more difficult. The was no girls' grammar school in the town but the council seemed loath to provide more than the barest minimum of secondary education for girls. The result was the opening of a pupil teacher centre in the unused upper story of St Helen's School in October 1906.

During its short life the centre appears to have served the dual role of training girls aged fourteen to eighteen to become women teachers for Hastings schools, and also acting as the first secondary school for girls in the town.[28] The Board of Education in London was unhappy about the scheme. Similar centres elsewhere in England were being closed down rather than opened up, and the Board only approved the centre as a temporary measure until a proper 'higher education' scheme was formulated.

By 1911 relationships with central government over the issue had worsened. The Board of Education refused to pay a grant until a proper secondary school for girls was provided. Although Hastings council tried to bluff the situation out, it was clear that it had no realistic choice but to close the centre and do as the Board wished. In 1911 an emergency committee of the education committee considered the issue and three alternatives for a site for a secondary school for girls: buying a new site and building a new school; buying and converting an existing building; using the St. Helen's building. The last

*Clive Vale School Christmas tea given by Mr and Mrs Arthur du Cros,
December 1909*

alternative was turned down by the emergency committee—it was
thought the Board of Education would not welcome it, and that the
site was too far from the town centre. In the event, however, this was
the option that was put into practice.

The elementary school using the ground floor of the St Helen's
building was closed, and Hastings Secondary School for Girls was
opened in October 1911. The headmistress was the former head of the
pupil teacher centre, Miss Nellie Clark. Her first annual report suggests
the change, at least from her point of view, was small. Examination
results of the seventy-four pupils at the school were not as good as
previous years, the blame being placed on the conversion to a
secondary school. The major changes seemed to have been the
introduction of swimming (thought to be unpopular because of the
cold summer) and school dinners (a condition imposed on the council
by the Board of Education if they were to accept the plan, and
threepence each for 'a hot roast meat, roast potatoes, several vegetables,
and in the summer an abundance of fruit'). The school was attended by
a combination of fee payers, girls on scholarships and bursaries, and
pupil teachers.

Mount Pleasant School children February 1910

In its early years the school prospered. There were 141 pupils by 1918. By the mid-1920s, however, attendances began to fall. In part this seems to have been linked to changes in the rest of the school system in Hastings.

The Education Act of 1918 was an expression of early post-war optimism; it swept away the remains of the Victorian education system. The school leaving age was raised to fourteen. The old half-time system was ended, and the employment of children under twelve prohibited (although it still went on unofficially). Fees in state schools—such as the Hastings Secondary School for Girls—were abolished. Teaching was given an increased professional status—salaries rose substantially, and the Burnham Committee (which was to survive until 1986) established to negotiate on pay.

Perhaps the biggest impact of the 1918 Act locally was that the education committee began to plan a more comprehensive system of education for children over the age of eleven. A variety of schemes were examined over the next few years.

The first suggestion was that in addition to the elite boys' grammar and girls' secondary there should be five 'central' schools for what were seen as the more 'intelligent' children and six 'senior' schools for the remainder. The scheme was then modified to provide for three central schools with 520 places. This scheme went no further due to the Government's economy campaign known as the Geddes Axe.

In 1924 another secondary education plan was drawn up. Two central schools would each cater for 250 pupils (or, if the school leaving age were fifteen, for 300 pupils). There were arguments about whether these schools should be mixed, or one for boys and the other for girls. Senior schools were to provide education for the remainder of children over eleven. Each would have places for 210 children, with children being divided into two grades.

A further more comprehensive report on secondary education in Hastings was published in early 1925.[29] This recommended the establishment of central or senior schools to provide suitable education for all children over eleven who did not go to a secondary school; increasing the proportion of trained teachers; the provision of another centre for laundry work and household management; and that organised games be developed.

As a result of the report and Board of Education pressure, a sub-committee of Hastings Education Committee produced a scheme[30] to establish a mixed central school at Tower Road, while at Priory Road there would be a central school for boys and a central school for girls. The scheme also divided the town into seven areas; in each there was provision for the education of infants and juniors, and in all except two areas there was provision for senior education for boys and girls. In some areas senior education was mixed and this led to complaints; at a meeting at the Town Hall many parents objected to 'a man teaching girl scholars'. To reduce criticism the education committee agreed that there would be separate playgrounds for boys and girls.

This scheme was carried through. The result, in 1926, was a substantial reorganisation and 'rationalisation' of schools in the town. Some schools lost departments, while others gained them. Elementary schools were retitled 'junior' schools. Older pupils went to either senior or central school, or to the grammar school for boys or secondary school for girls. These last two schools were thought of as the 'higher' educational provision in the town.

In just twenty-five years education for older children had emerged from almost nothing to be an important part of the local school system. In 1900 the vast majority of working class children had no chance of going to anything other than an elementary school—any other idea would have been unthinkable. By 1926 a secondary education system was in place. This system was, however, highly structured—going to a senior school was a very different experience than going to Hastings Grammar.

This 'educational revolution'[31] included the building of laboratories and improvement of libraries in the central schools, and in one case 'a school journey to France to supplement ... teaching of French'. It was even accepted that the previous system of the borough training its own teachers 'had led to some degree of educational stagnation'.

By the late-1920s the problems of the girls' secondary school had grown. Once again the education committee looked at the option of a new building on a different site. Once again the option was turned down. Instead the secondary school was renamed, becoming the Hastings High School for Girls in September 1929. For once, the introduction of the high school was at the front of (rather than behind) national trends. The image of the old St Helen's buildings was improved: the asphalt and Victorian iron railings were replaced by a garden with rockery and grass. Whether because of the rockery or not, the school did attract more pupils; in 1930 there were nearly 200. By

1936 a new music room and laboratory had been built (a decade after an extension was first mooted).

Poverty and Health

Throughout the nineteenth century and first part of this century two persistent themes in the evolution of education in Hastings were poverty and health. In general, the poorest children received the worst education at the most inadequate schools. Poverty interfered with education in a number of ways. It was the poorest children who were most likely not to attend school because of ill-health, hunger, the need to work, the pressure of family and friends, or even because they had no boots to wear despite snow on the ground. At worst poverty was the death of children. This section looks at poverty and health amongst Hastings children from the late nineteenth century, particularly from the viewpoint of the town council's key medical officers.

During the last quarter of the nineteenth century health care was in its infancy. Hygiene was practically unknown and a great number of people, particularly infants in their first year of life, died from diseases that were largely preventable. Children born to large poor families were more at risk than those born into the better-off home. Most families expected to lose at least one child in infancy. The highest risk of all was to the illegitimate child. Smallpox and diptheria were still common diseases and epidemics of measles, whooping cough and croup could kill a lot of pre-school children particularly those who were poorly nourished and with little resistance to fight off infection. School logbooks say much about the situation. For example, from the log of St Clement's School, Halton, for April 1869: 'Measles and Throat disease amongst the children, two little ones died within the week'.

But the worst diseases of all—if only because they were completely preventable with reasonable standards of hygiene—were diarrhoea and dysentery. In some years more infants died from these than from all other diseases put together. Reporting on the year 1878, Dr Ashenden says 'As usual, the mortality amongst children is very great. No less a number than 227 died under five years of age, being one-third of the total deaths from all causes. One hundred and thirty six of these were infants under one year of age'.

The Medical Officers of Health, Dr Ashenden and later Dr A. Scarlyn Wilson were, judging from their reports, conscientious men who worked hard to improve the general health of all the townspeople, pressing the council to provide the facilities to keep infectious diseases at bay. The council of a town that saw itself as a 'health resort' could not afford to look niggardly on health care, particularly in comparison with other towns. On the other hand, the ratepayer lobby, well represented on the council, had a very conservative approach to local public expenditure.

Dr Ashenden got 'a disinfecting apparatus' and 'Sanitary cart' after continually pointing out in his reports that the purchase of these items would save money in the long run. At that time all infected bedding and clothing had to be destroyed and the—usually very poor—owners reimbursed. In the early days the council made a yearly grant of fifty guineas to the St Leonards Sanitorium and infectious cases from Hastings were sent there, but in each yearly report Dr Ashenden begged for 'An infection hospital of our own' stressing that 'it would give confidence to the public'. Fortunately this appeal was sanctioned by October 1875—in the following month 'two cases of smallpox were imported into the borough. Immediate steps were taken to isolate these at the rooms provided at Gensing Road ... but we could not stay the spread of this loathsome disease and fifteen more cases quickly followed in different parts of the western borough'. The Sanitary Committee purchased an appropriate building immediately which did much to curtail the spread of the epidemic and by 26th February 1876, Dr Ashenden was able to report that there had been no fresh case for six weeks. Three people died in the outbreak, one of them being a visitor to Hastings of two days standing, having brought the disease (from Eastbourne) in the first place.

In 1885 there were bad epidemics of smallpox and scarlet fever at the same time. The situation so badly strained the resources of the sanitorium that one of the 'Humphreys Temporary Iron Hospitals' was erected on a site next to the hospital. The ninety scarlet fever patients were transferred to it, so isolating the two diseases from each other which had previously not been completely possible. 'Unfortunately instances have occurred of attendants, and others, contracting smallpox from this cause.' There were 134 cases of scarlet fever in all but no deaths. Six people died from smallpox including three children aged five years, five months and eighteen days. This epidemic ran over into the first six weeks of the next year and there was one more death. There was also a sharp epidemic of measles the same year from which twenty-five died, only three being over five years old.

This seems to have been the last epidemic of smallpox in Hastings. In 1892 the then MOH, Dr A. Scarlyn Wilson, reported that there had not been a case of smallpox for seven years, although in view of the fact that there had been outbreaks in other parts of the country, an outlying farm was kept in case there was need for isolation.

Until 1907 there was no separate medical provision for schools and children—the MOH had responsibility for all aspects of health care. Following the election of the reforming Liberal Government, in 1907 the Board of Education issued a circular, 'On Medical Inspection of Children in Elementary Schools', which stipulated that there should be a School Medical Officer whose sole employment would be the care of schoolchildren of the borough.

In Hastings the council wanted to use five doctors already in practice in the various rather spread out districts of the town. This was not allowed by the Board in London. Dr Oliver Polhill Turner was duly appointed to enter into his duties in December 1908 and commenced actual inspections in February 1909. The number of children on the school registers was 8,610 and Dr Turner managed to see 1,881.

Results of the examinations showed a considerable amount of disease and defect in the children. A large number of cases were dealt with at hospitals and dispensaries and by private medical practitioners. But there were some difficulties in obtaining treatment especially for 'necessitous children' suffering from minor ailments. It was therefore decided in 1911 that a school clinic should be set up, and a school nurse had already been appointed.

In 1913 Dr Turner presented a very comprehensive report covering even such aspects of school life as improvements to buildings. The work of the school clinics had grown to such an extent that, although three school nurses were now employed, they could not cope with the full volume of work that Dr Turner would have liked. The death rate from infectious diseases had declined steadily over the previous decade and time was now given to dealing with dirt-related conditions such as ringworm, running ears and sore eyes.

There were considerable numbers of children with verminous heads, bodies and clothing. They were treated at the cleansing station at Rock-a-Nore, probably often being dipped like sheep. It must have been a thankless task because many of the children would have been re-infested within a short time. The school nurses did visit the homes of verminous and neglected children, and in most cases the attitude of the

Boys outside Halton Parish Room holding basins of porridge, part of their free breakfasts, November 1910

parents was 'courteous and civil'. They seemed glad of the advice.

Dr Turner was anxious for the school nurses to visit the homes of pre-school children, particularly during epidemics of measles and whooping cough which might be brought home by older children at school, to advise mothers regarding the care of such cases. Although these were not notifiable diseases the mortality was often high among young children and the majority of parents were inclined to consider them as trivial complaints.

Dr Turner considered that Hastings was unique for its combination of school clinics and Institutes for Motherhood and Infancy, the income for the latter being derived from a few philanthropic people. When infants ceased to attend they frequently deteriorated.

Presumably partly on the basis of his work and experiences in Hastings, Dr Turner advocated far-reaching and radical changes to child care in Britain. He states 'There is no doubt that the most satisfactory method of dealing with the matter would be for the Local Education Authorities to take over the child life of the country, starting with the expectant mothers, and be responsible for the child until it leaves school. Although the state aid of such Institutions would mean more expenditure, nevertheless, experience tends to prove it would really mean economy in the long run, and would also allow such Institutions to widen their scope of usefulness as regards providing sterilised milk, the medical treatment of children under school age etc., in fact carrying out a practical method of raising healthy stock, which is, undoubtedly, not only the most potent method of preventing disease, but also of improving the national health'.

These extreme views about the role of the state in childhood were not taken further in Hastings. However, very similar arguments were made in the town during the Second World War.

Hastings council, or at least its health officials were, then, going some way to provide health care of poor children. As the accounts in part one show, not everyone always turned to the council for help, and people often made use of chemists, unofficial midwives, and so on. Another key area of poverty and health was the question of lack of food. This was closely related to what at the time was seen as the major problem known as 'physical deterioration' of the working class. At first Hastings council did little itself to alleviate hunger, leaving it to charities to provide what they could. The best example here is the work of the Ore penny dinner fund established in the 1880s.

THE KURSAAL,

PALACE PIER, ST. LEONARDS.

—Programme—

OF

GRAND

Bohemian Concert

IN AID OF THE

POOR CHILDREN'S BOOT FUND

—ON—

Monday, March 25th, 1912,

At 8 p.m.

THE RIGHT WORSHIPFUL THE MAYOR,

(G. HUTCHINGS, Esq., J.P.)

WILL PRESIDE.

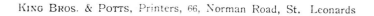

KING BROS. & POTTS, Printers, 66, Norman Road, St. Leonards

In 1906, however, with the Education (Provision of Meals) Act the council was given the legal powers to provide school meals out of rates if it so wished. Despite clear evidence of the need—head teachers estimated that in the winter of 1907 there were 354 'children who attend school in want of food'[33]—at first the education committee did nothing, trying to push the problem on to existing charities and the Poor Law Guardians. Intense pressure mounted,[34] however, from individual committee members and such diverse groups as Hastings and St Leonards Charity Organisation Society, the Guardians of Hastings Poor Law Union, the Hastings branch of the Independent Labour Party, and the Social Democratic Federation. Eventually, in January 1908 the education committee agreed to provide breakfasts for 'necessitous children' during the winter.

Once established, free meals became an important feature of the work of the education committee. During the winter of 1912-1913 meals were provided in Ore, Old Town, Halton, Silverhill and Hollington, and West St Leonards. 59,333 free breakfasts were given at a cost of 1.54d (food only) per meal, the total cost for food being £381.0.4d During the year 1913, 2,041 free lunches were given at a total cost of £9.9.7d. On Monday, Tuesday and Thursday the

Some of the 200 children from Sandown School after having their free breakfasts in November 1911

breakfasts consisted of a half pint of oatmeal porridge with a third of a pint of new milk and one ounce of demerara sugar, and two slices (5 oz) of bread and butter, dripping or jam. On Wednesday and Friday the breakfasts consisted of bread and milk with sugar and bread and butter or dripping.

Old people in the town remember that to qualify for the breakfasts they had to get to school on time when they would be given a token for the next day's breakfast, but according to Dr Turner the parents had to fill in a form obtained from the local attendance officer and return this to the education committee offices. Dr Turner sampled the breakfasts and found them palatable but suggested more dripping in place of jam, as more nutritious and children preferred it.

The voluntary funded Ore penny dinners, which had been in existence for over thirty years, continued despite the work of the council. During the winter of 1912–13, 12,626 dinners were served, more than 900 weekly, at a cost of £73.2.8d. During the previous twenty years more than 260,000 had been given. Polhill Turner reported that since work was particularly scarce in Ore during the winter, many children would suffer considerably if it were not for the penny dinner fund.

Another dimension of poverty was lack of reasonable boots or shoes. A decade into the twentieth century, a number of 'boot funds' to provide footwear for needy children existed. One was set up in 1908, with assistance from some headteachers and friends, by the secretary to the education committee. By the end of 1913 1,738 pairs had been provided. A further boot fund started in 1909 when the National Union of Teachers, whose annual conference met in the town, raised £150 and an anonymous donor gave £200. These monies had been invested to produce £12.6.2d yearly. Yet another boot fund was run by the police.

Not everyone accepted that poverty was the major cause of hunger, inadequate clothing, and poor housing. T.S. Dymond, mayor of Hastings in 1926–27, thought 'cases of malnutrition of children are as often due to the ignorance and thriftlessness of the mothers as poverty'.[35] The evidence of people who lived through the period as children does not bear this statement out.

Sometimes health followed national trends. In 1900 the birthrate in

Winkle Club Christmas Dinner 1912

the borough was unprecedentedly low, as it was in the whole of the UK. The absence of a considerable number of men fighting the Boer War was considered to be the reason for this. However, during the First World War the number of illegitimate babies increased enormously. No doubt this was because there were a great number of troops billeted in the town.

In 1916 the annual report (rather brief) was made by the secretary to the education committee because Dr Turner was on war duty. Local doctors worked part-time at the clinics and the school nurses coped with the rest. If there were outbreaks of infectious diseases the MOH visited the schools. It was a bad year for diptheria, with the highest number of cases for many years.

In 1918 there was a serious outbreak of influenza and only one school remained open. Several infants schools were closed because of measles and there was also a considerable attack of scabies. Schools in the Old Town and also Sandown School, were closed while children were treated and the schools cleansed. The parasite had been brought by soldiers home on leave.

During this time needy children were being supplied with tonics and supplements such as cod liver oil and Virol through by the school clinics. Medicines and dressings were also supplied and spectacles, and sundries (including soap). Meals were still being provided.

In 1923 the school medical service was absorbed into the general health department. Dr Turner, although carrying on the same work, was now known as 'Deputy School Medical Officer'. In 1924 the report looked forward to the provision of an open air school for delicate children and those with non-infectious tuberculosis and also 'an orthopaedic scheme to deal completely with our crippled children'. The next couple of years saw both these schemes come to fruition.

All the time the school medical service was growing and needing more staff. The educational efforts of the service seems to have had some long term effect. The incidence of ringworm, impetigo, scabies and similar diseases was lessening. In 1925 the MOH thought 'Fortunately the gross conditions of uncleanliness which were by no means uncommon in the schools some 15 years ago, have now ceased to exist. At the same time, it is essential for the nursing staff to pay frequent visits to the schools for inspections and to impress upon the parents the need for absolute cleanliness'.

All through the twenties and thirties meals (from 1920 dinner rather than breakfast) were provided during the winter for needy children, although now they were provided by the cheaper sort of restaurant which were glad to have the trade during the slack winter season. The menu included such items as steak and kidney pudding with potatoes and peas; roast beef with Yorkshire pudding, potatoes and peas; fried sausages with mashed potatoes and onions, followed by apple pudding; stewed mutton and beef with turnips and potatoes; and, liver and bacon, potatoes and cabbage followed by plain currant pudding. Puddings were not provided every day, but it was stipulated that only new milk and fresh English meat were to be used.

From about 1922 free milk was provided to a limited number of very debilitated children—the number increasing each year. By 1926 the children were getting a half pint of milk with biscuits or bread and butter and Dr Turner was beginning to monitor their weight gain. However, Dr Turner died in 1927 and this scheme was held up for a time, but in 1929 the new School Medical Officer was able to report an average gain in weight between six and seven pounds, and in one case eleven pounds, and a corresponding improvement in general health. In the 1930s under a scheme run by the Milk Marketing Board bottles of a third of a pint of milk were sold in schools cheaply to those who wanted it, although needy children still had theirs free.

By 1936 school meals were provided throughout the year for needy children. During the warmer months the School Medical Officer arranged for lighter meals, salads, sweets and stewed fruit. Children did not like this food, preferring the heavier winter menus. By this time the general overall health of the majority of children was good. Great strides in hygiene had cut the death rate of new born babies; skin diseases, such a large part of the work of the early clinics, were much less; and vaccination had cut down the cases of diptheria and tuberculosis considerably. Of course the children who had experienced the gradual increase in health care over the last thirty years were parents themselves now, and they knew a thing or two their parents had to learn painfully.

World War Two and the Future

From the turn of the century for almost four decades there was gradual educational progress in Hastings. Although sometimes unwillingly and only because of local and central government pressure, Hastings council now provided a comprehensive education and welfare service for local children. The school leaving age had risen, a system of secondary education was in place, school meals were available, and a good school health service was in operation. By 1939 there were plans for new girls' and boys' 'modern schools', proposals for similar schools in St Leonards, and a new infants' school and an open air school were under construction at Red lake. But all this progress was under a greater threat than ever before, that of the looming Second World War.

Initially it was assumed that as with the First War Hastings would not be in the front line. Instead the town became a reception area for children evacuated from London (some expectant mothers and others with children under school age were also evacuated). The first London children arrived on 1 September 1939, two days before Britain declared war on Germany. The nearly 3,000 children were bussed to various schools in Hastings which they were to share with local children. The London children were billeted as far as possible in the neighbourhood of their new schools. Once the Hastings children returned from their summer holidays, lessons were given on a shift system, London children being taught by their own teachers.[36]

To occupy the children outside the classroom they were taken on organised rambles and games were organised against teams of local children. Mr I.T. Hopkins of Mount Pleasant Schools, a prominent figure in schoolboy soccer in Hastings for many years, appealed for assistance in running the matches which were played on the grounds of local clubs on Saturday mornings.[37]

In December 1939 school children from Deptford were visited by their mayor at Hastings Boys' Central School and the West St Leonards School. The mayor also visited Westfield, where girls from one Deptford school were billeted.[38] The girls of Hastings High School shared the buildings with 255 pupils from St Ursula's High School, Greenwich.

In December 1939 Hastings church leaders met twenty-seven London headteachers at St Leonards parish church hall to discuss the problem of entertaining the evacuees during Christmas. The meeting resulted in at least ten entertainments per week over the festive period—these included stage shows, films and conjurors.[39] By the end of December 1939 about a third of the London evacuees had returned home, at the end of the year there were 2,087 still registered as attending school in Hastings.[40]

In June 1940, following the Dunkirk evacuation and the French capitulation, it was becoming clear that Hastings was not such a safe place, and that it might end up in the front line. All London school children left Hastings, and it was now the turn of Hastings school children to be evacuated. In July 3,000 Hastings school children, about fifty per cent of the town's school population, were evacuated to Bedfordshire and Hertfordshire. They joined up with pupils from London schools already there. Other local children went to South Wales. The children left Hastings by train, each child identified by a label tied to their clothing. One report describes them waiting to board trains, 'in addition to carrying their gasmasks and little suitcases, also sandwiches, most of them were carrying toys, dolls, footballs, cricket bats and other juvenile treasures'.[41]

This situation created problems about whether it would be possible for Hastings school children to remain with their own teachers. Some Hastings headteachers became assistant teachers serving under London headteachers. The central schools merged to become a mixed central school under Mr Read and Miss Button. The Girls High School worked on a shift system with a local girls grammar school and a London school. The special schools hired one of the boarding houses of an 'important and modern Midland School' and worked with their own staff. The Open Air School was housed in a hostel which was used entirely for residential purposes; lessons were given in the grandstand of a football ground.[42] In August 1940 a large unfurnished country mansion was given by a noted financier for the use of Hastings schoolchildren, which was equipped as a sort of boarding school for Ore Infants School.[43]

All schools in Hastings were closed, but as not all children were evacuated there was need of fewer teachers in the reception areas. The education committee wanted to reduce the number of teachers from 210 to 137. It aimed to do this by sacking all supply teachers and terminating the contracts of all teachers over sixty and of all married teachers who had someone to support them financially.[44]

As the threat of German invasion receded by the end of 1940, people started to agitate for the reopening of schools in Hastings and other towns along the south coast. There was a fear that children in Hastings were becoming illiterate.[45] There were several private schools open in Hastings at the end of 1940. It may have been this factor which persuaded the Board of Education to sanction the opening of schools not only in Hastings but also in Newhaven, Seaford, Eastbourne and Bexhill, provided that each school had sufficient air raid shelters

conforming to the ARP code. It was this which was mainly responsible for the delay in reopening schools in Hastings. Most had virtually no air raid shelter provision because, until June 1940, Hastings had been a reception area and as such had not been allowed to obtain materials for air raid shelters.[46]

The education committee decided to reopen Ore and Silverhill schools once their shelters had been completed and their windows protected by wire netting. In April 1941 provision was made for part-time education in Hastings. Eight schools where the air raid precautions were adequate were opened for two shifts of children each. In districts where a school was open attendance was compulsory for all children over the age of five. However places could not be found in these schools for children who returned to the district after the middle of April. It was not possible to re-establish compulsory education in the whole town as twelve schools were suffering from war damage and some schools were being used for other purposes. It was decided to provide out-of-school activities, games, PT and practical pursuits to fill the hours when children could not be in the classroom. Some staff were to be recalled from the reception areas.[47]

By June 1941 there were far more children of school age in Hastings than there were Hastings children in the reception areas (2,959 and 1,685 respectively). But there were eighty-nine Hastings teachers in the reception areas, and only thirty-two in Hastings itself. At Ore Boys School three masters had care of 196 boys, and one mistress at Priory Road Infants School was responsible for forty-eight children.[48]

By 1940 the life of many children who remained in the town was radically changed. Many did not go to school. Parents worked long hours or were perhaps even away from home for weeks or months on end. The homes of some children were bombed. In the Old Town use was made of St Clements Caves, not simply as air raid shelters, but in some cases as an almost permanent home. Communal feeding centres became an established feature of life in the town.

Some people thought that such developments would continue after the War. The organiser of one communal feeding centre thought: 'Communal feeding has an educational value, too, that shows great promise .... It used to be difficult to gain contact between the home and

'Somewhere in Hertfordshire', pupils of the Cavendish Place School, October 1940

'Cave Dwellers in South-East Town', November 1940

the school—to know the parents as well as the children. But now the parents come to lunch we chat with them, and the result will be closer co-operation between home and school than ever before .... Communal feeding has come to stay—not just for the duration, but as a permanent feature of local life.'[49]

Other people agreed. The authoress and playwright, Clemence Dane, argued communal feeding was 'going to become as much a part of our English life as the police service, and it supplies us with the right which everybody owns, the right to have decent food in decent surroundings at a price he or she could afford to pay ... Hastings is a pattern which other towns should copy.'[50] Clemence Dane did not, however, like the word 'communal' and suggested 'Everyman's Inn' or 'National Inn' instead.

Two weeks after this view was reported the local Conservative MP hit back against such radical ideas. In a speech made in March 1941, Hely-Hutchinson argued: 'I feel bound to say, while acknowledging that training and certain aspects of upbringing are best ... achieved by co-operative methods ... nothing can replace the background provided for a child's upbringing and training by the strength, shelter and privacy of home and family life. The unit of life is not the individual, but the family; and the privacy of home and family life is the foundation of the English character .... The head of the family is above the state.'[51]

Even in 1943 Hastings could not regarded as safe. In air raids on 11

March Halton and St Matthews Schools were damaged so badly that the education committee decided to ask the Board of Education for permission to demolish the damaged buildings, clear the sites and prepare the way for the erection of new buildings of modern pattern after the war.[52] On 7 July a further meeting decided to delay a decision on the future of these schools until the far reaching Butler Education Bill became law.[53]

By this stage thoughts were turning to the future and education nationally and locally after the War. A report on 'Post War Education' was presented to the education committee by a special sub-committee on 20 October 1943. It recommended that a survey be made of existing school premises to determine what part they could play in providing adequate facilities for primary education. It also recommended that immediate steps should be taken to acquire a site and prepare building plans for a modern school in St Leonards; that existing plans for a modern school at Red Lake should be reconsidered; that plans be prepared for adapting and extending Priory Road and Tower Road schools for 'modern school' purposes; and, preliminary enquiries be made for a site for new premises for the art and science schools as a nucleus of a future municipal college.

This sub-committee produced another report in July 1944, which looked at the implications for Hastings of the new Education Act. Under the Act, education was organised in three 'progressive stages to be known as primary education, secondary education, and further education'. In turn, secondary education was to be divided into three types—grammar schools, technical schools and secondary modern schools. It was pointed out by the sub-committee that by April 1946 the local education authority had to prepare a development plan for the education of all those below the age of fifteen, which would be submitted to the newly created Minister of Education. By 1 April 1948 Hastings would also have to establish and maintain a 'young people's college' for part-time education of 15-18 year olds.

As a general policy the committee recommended that nursery classes for children under the age of five should be held in infants' schools, nursery schools were to be established only in exceptional circumstances. Infants' schools were to be separate units under their own Headmistress, although where numbers were low infants were to be attached to junior schools.

The committee also considered plans for extending the premises of the High School which, like the Grammar School, might under the new Act have to cater for more pupils and a wider curriculum. It was planned to establish four secondary modern schools in the town: one for boys at Priory Road; one for girls at Tower Road (at both these schools the existing buildings would need to be enlarged) one girls' school on a site already acquired at Red Lake; and a boys' school on a site to be chosen in the Western part of the town.

As the War ended and the Butler Act came into force, children and parents in Hastings could look forward to a major reorganisation of the school system in the town, the school leaving age going up to fifteen, and, for the first time, a legal entitlement to school meals and free milk to be provided by the local authority.

VE Day celebrations in Boyne Road

NOTES

1. See the bibliography at the end of part three, Hastings school directory.
2. A comprehensive account of the changing nature of schools and education in England as a whole is provided by J. Lawson and H. Silver (1973) *A Social History of Education in England.*
3. *A Digest of Parochial Returns Made to the Select Committee Appointed to Inquire into the Education of the Poor. Part II England* (1818).
4. J. Manwaring Banes (1986, revised edition) *Historic Hastings.*
5. *School Inquiry Commission Special Report by Assistant Commissioners (Vol XI) South-Eastern Division, 1867–68, Vol XXVIII, Part IX.*
6. B. Funnell (1972) *A History of Christ Church School 1872–1972.*
7. *Hastings and St Leonards Chronicle,* 8 January 1871. The survey excluded Ore.
8. See note 5.
9. *Hastings and St Leonards Chronicle,* 17 May 1871.
10. *Hastings and St Leonards News,* 3 June 1859.
11. *Hastings and St Leonards News,* 20 December 1855.
12. Lawson and Silver, *op.cit.*
13. *Hastings and St Leonards Chronicle,* June 7 1871.
14. A full account is provided in B. Lawes (1987) *Helenswood School and its Origins 1870–1987.*
15. Hastings (U.D.) School Board (1901) *Triennial Report 1898–1900.*
16. For an account of Bristol see S. Humphries (1983) 'Radical childhood (1889–1939)', in Bristol Broadsides, *Bristol's Other History.*
17. Hastings Modern History Workshop (1983) *A History of Ore to 1914.*
18. Hastings (U.D.) School Board (1901) *Triennial Report 1898–1900.*
19. See Lawson and Silver, *op.cit.*
20. *Hastings and St Leonards Weekly Times,* 23 April 1904.
21. *Hastings Corporation Education Committee Minutes (HCECM),* Vol. 1, p 252.
22. *Ibid.,* p 267.
23. *Ibid.,* Vol. 4, pp 22–3.
24. *Ibid.,* Vol. 1, pp 137–8 and 155.
25. *Ibid.,* pp 8–9.
26. *Ibid.,* Vol. 5, pp 65–6.

27. *Ibid.*, pp 140–1.
28. For a full account see B. Lawes, *op.cit.*
29. *Hastings and St Leonards Observer*, 14 March 1925.
30. *Hastings and St Leonards Observer*, 18 July 1925.
31. So called by T.S. Diamond mayor of Hastings 1926–27 in his 1928 book *The Memoirs of a Mayor of Hastings.*
32. Unless otherwise stated, information in this section is drawn from the annual reports of the MOH and the School Medical Officer.
33. *HCECM*, Volume 4, p 201.
34. *Ibid.*, pp 202–3, 212, 218–9, 225, 227, 247, 250–1.
35. *op.cit.*, p 108.
36. *Hastings and St Leonards Observer*, 2 September 1939.
37. *Ibid.*, 30 September 1939.
38. *Ibid.*, 9 December 1939.
39. *Ibid.*, 16 December 1939.
40. *HCECM*, 26 January 1940.
41. *Hastings and St Leonards Observer*, 27 July 1940.
42. *Ibid.*
43. *Ibid.*, 10 August 1940.
44. *HCECM*, 27 November 1940.
45. *Hastings and St Leonards Observer*, 4 January 1941.
46. *Ibid.*
47. *HCECM*, 16 April 1941.
48. *Ibid.*, 25 June 1941.
49. *Hastings and St Leonards Observer*, 23 November 1940.
50. *Ibid.*, 15 February 1941.
51. *Ibid.*, 1 March 1941
52. *HCECM.*, 21 April 1943.
53. *Ibid.*, 1 July 1943.

Part Three
Hastings School Directory

HASTINGS SCHOOL DIRECTORY

This alphabetical list gives details of schools in Hastings and St Leonards during the years 1870 to 1945. It excludes all obviously private schools, except for those which eventually became part of the 'state' sector. It also includes information about the earlier and more recent history of schools in the town. We have tried to make this school directory as comprehensive as possible, but there are gaps and we would be grateful for further information for future editions. If you can help please contact the Hastings Modern History Workshop, c/o Steve Peak, 18 Plynlimmon Road, Hastings.

The list is organised as follows: Name of school; date of opening (and closure, if appropriate)
Address
Other information

ALL SAINTS SCHOOL; 1835-present
Various locations.
Initially also known as Hastings National School and All Saints and St Clements National Schools. Opened 18 November for boys and girls (with a fee of one penny per child weekly) in building at 57 All Saints Street given by Countess Waldegrave on strict understanding that there would be separate entrances for boys and girls. This building survives. 1853 a new separate school for girls opened in All Saints Street (now demolished, on the site of the flats at 99–100 All Saints Street). 1864 infants' school opened, no child admitted under age of two and pupils transferred to the National Schools at 6. By 1871 boys' school in Tackleway (now Tackleway Boys' Club). 1913 moved to Harold Road with 171 boys and 52 girls. On re-organisation in 1926 became a Junior Mixed and Infants' school. 1959 the school, with 265 pupils, moved to Githa Road (into part of the former Clive Vale School) and the Harold Road building became Dudley Infants School.

BOPEEP SCHOOL; 1866-1898
Address (?)
Also known as the St Leonards Bopeep National Infants' School. A Church of England voluntary school, established by Rev. J. Awdry Jamieson in a building belonging to the Railway Company for a nominal rent of £1 a year. On closure the children were transferred to the new West St Leonards Infants Board School.

BOURNE WALK SCHOOL; 1863-1891

Bourne Walk

Also known as the Hastings Boys' British School, although transferred to and part of Hastings School Board in the early 1870s. 1874 William Ray master, with two pupil teachers. 1877 premises described as 'inconvenient and insanitary in the highest degree'. Windows could not be opened because 'of the stench outside'. There was no playground. 1877–1882 William Evans headmaster (he was transferred to Mount Pleasant School). 1882–1924 L.J. Jukes headmaster. Numbers increased from 150 to 333. 1891 moved to new premises in Priory Road, and became Priory Road School. Building subsequently fitted out for woodwork instruction for boys from various schools and for evening classes, eventually becoming part of Hastings Technical College. Buildings are now demolished.

CAVENDISH PLACE SCHOOL; 1829-

Cavendish Place and Croft Road

Opened 22 June, as part of the Infant School Society, for children 2 to 7. Fee of twopence per child per week. 'Parents are to send their children well washed and combed, with their hair cut short, and their clothes neat and clean, by half-past eight o'clock in the morning.' April 1898 Alice Turner started as headmistress. 1918 non-provided school with 129 places, average attendance 41. Building now houses the Hastings and district Scout headquarters.

CHRIST CHURCH SCHOOL; c.1860-present

Alfred Street.

Initially an infants only school in rented accommodation at 20 Alfred Street, Miss T. Moon the mistress-in-charge. By 1869 girls (but not boys) of all ages could attend. 1873 new school building completed at a cost of £2300 next to church, lower floor for 200 infants, first floor schools for boys and girls (220 in total), upper floor rooms for teachers. There was no playground, children drilling in Alfred Street. c.1895 disused British School on opposite side of London Road used as overflow boys' school. 1896 new boys' school opened, on top of original church and parish room. 1926 on re-organisation of education in Hastings became an infant and junior school, the older pupils going to either Tower Road or St Leonards School.

CLIVE VALE SCHOOL; 1886-1957

Githa Road.
Opened as an infant school for 220 children, with Miss Rodney as headmistress. Major extension costing £7050 opened 26 February 1892, with accommodation for 276 boys and 276 girls. 'Each department comprises a large central hall and six class-rooms.' The building, by then occupied by Clive Vale Secondary Modern School, was closed in 1957, the boys joining Hastings Secondary Boys' School (Priory Road) and the girls Hastings Secondary Girls' School (Rye Road). c.1959 lower floor re-occupied by All Saints School, upper floor became an annex of Hastings Secondary Boys' until 1979.

HALTON SCHOOL; 1838/40-1943

Egremont Place/Albion Street.
The original National School largely paid for by Mrs Sarah Milward (later the Countess of Waldegrave) who also provided the land. In November 1858 she promised a further £500 (if matched by public donations of £150) to build 'an infant school room, amply sufficient to meet both the present and also any probable future necessities of the parish, and to combine with it a suitable dwelling-house for the residence of the mistress'. The extension, for 160 children, was opened the following year. The Rev. John Parkin, MA, Vicar of Halton Church for 49 years, was an important force behind the building and development of the school. 1871 76 boys, 67 girls, 50 infant boys and 49 infant girls. 1878 new boys' school opened. 1894 infants' again needed extending. 1895 gallery to be built in babies' (infants') room at a cost of £800. 1905 following Government inspection a new boys' school built, a separate entrance provided for the infants, and the playground doubled in size. The school was bombed during the Second War, the estimated cost of rebuilding being £24,000, and it was never rebuilt.

HAROLD ROAD SCHOOL

See All Saints School.

HASTINGS BOYS BRITISH SCHOOL; 1840-1891

Wellington Square and Bourne Walk.
Founded in September 1840 in a room under the Baptist Chapel, Wellington Square, for 150 boys. Voluntary subscription of twopence per boy weekly. Master may have been John Wise. 1853 first public exam. 1854 Theophilus Urry master. 1857 William King master. 1863

land purchased in Cobourg Place for new school. Residents objected, one trustee remarking 'People are often more sensitive to the nuisance of a school near them than they are to a beershop or public house'. In same year new school erected in Bourne Walk, north of Waterloo Passage and Saunders School and at the rear of 9 High Street. 1870s subjects limited to grammar, geography, handwriting, singing, reading, composition, arthmetic, and spelling. 1875 taken over by Hastings School Board. See Bourne Walk School.

HASTINGS GIRLS BRITISH SCHOOL; 1835-
Waterloo Passage.
Founded in the old Wesleyan Chapel, under the patronage of the Duchess of Kent.

HASTINGS GRAMMAR SCHOOL; 1639-
Various locations

1639 school set up at top of High Street in house known as 'the School House' or 'the Stone House', on the site of the present Torfield House, with money from rents of property left in the will of Rev. William Parker, Rector of All Saints Church. 1708/9 school set up under will of James Saunders. 1809 both schools managed by one master, Joseph Hannay. Rented room over ropemaker's shop on Rope Walk, now Robertson Terrace. 1813 after court case the two foundations separated. Saunders school ran into financial difficulties and the boys transferred to Parker's. 1817 Parker's school moved to site of what is now 16–20 Croft Road. 1818 Saunders' school re-started in one of the Breeds warehouses. 1822 new building erected for Saunders' in Bourne Walk. 1825 Parker's moved to over Thwaites grocery shop, parish of All Saints. 1848 John Banks, master of Parker's, built house and schoolroom attached at the top of Stonefield Road (now the Gospel Hall). 1878 both charities merged and, with part of Magdalen Charities, became one body, the Hastings Grammar School Foundation. This move was controversial because the Magdalen Charities were originally for the education and benefit of children from the parishes of All Saints and St Clements, where many of the poorest children in the town lived. Although several free places were to be offered, some people thought Old Town children would not benefit by the merger. 1880 new school formally opened, still in Banks' schoolroom. 1881 6 September, foundation stone laid in Nelson Road (then containing only about a dozen houses) for first proper school. 1883 4 July, new building formally opened. 1888–1913 William La Touche headmaster. 1913–35

P.S. Barlow headmaster making many humanizing changes such as flowers and pictures in classrooms. 1923 two houses added to existing three. 1932 350 boys. 1936 M.G.G. Hyder headmaster. 1939 after September numbers reach 480, swollen by evacuees. 1940 21 July school evacuated to St Albans (280 boys). In 1964 the school moved to new premises in parkstone Road, becoming William Parker School in 1978.

HASTINGS HIGH SCHOOL FOR GIRLS; 1929-1978
The Ridge.
See Hastings Secondary School for Girls. On opening as the High School, the old buildings given facelift, including removal of ashphalt and iron railings and their replacement by flower beds and a rockery. Victorian building demolished and replaced by new building opened in 1970. Became part of the new Helenswood Comprehensive School in 1978.

HASTINGS RAGGED SCHOOL
39a Tackleway.
Built about 1840 as a hall for All Saints Church. 1871 49 boys and 48 girls. Now an artist's studio.

HASTINGS SECONDARY MODERN SCHOOL FOR BOYS
See Priory Road School.

HASTINGS SECONDARY SCHOOL FOR GIRLS; 1911-1929
The Ridge. Opened in premises formerly used as St Helen's Mixed and Infants' School. First head Miss Nellie Clark, B.A. 65 pupils in first year of opening, rising to 141 by 1918. By late 1920s number of pupils declining, and the Education Committee converted the school into Hastings High School for Girls from September 1929.

HOLLINGTON SCHOOL; c.1854-1974
various locations.
Original National School seems to have been the upper floor of a cow shed behind 'Rock Cottage', Battle Road. New buildings in Old Church Lane opened January 18 1857 at a cost of £338, the money being raised by subscription and the land (outside the town boundary) given by the Beauport Estate. 1859 John Harmer master, Mary Harmer mistress. On establishment of the School Board in 1870, building used solely as a Sunday school, and in 1931 was sold and converted into two semi-detached houses known as 'Old School Cottages'. By 1871 an

infant school with 24 boys and 39 girls existed in Hollington Old Lane, rented for £5 from a local builder, Mr W.L. Langridge. By 1872 girls and infants educated separately from the boys. The original purpose-built Board girls' school (opened 1872) was in Battle Road/Hollington Old Lane. 1872 boys 'in a small school at Ald. Stone's gate'. 1876 boys occupied St John's Sunday School premises until 1880 and opening of purpose-built boys' school in Wishing Tree Road/Old Church Road at a cost £384 for the land and £1400 for building school and master's house. By 1918 a 'Special School' for 'mentally defective' children established in this buiding, the boys moving to Battle Road. This latter building was demolished in 1974. The Wishing Tree Road building is now used by Hollington Community Centre.

HOLY TRINITY SCHOOL; 1868-
Cambridge Road and Braybrooke Terrace.
Day school started in December 1868 by Dr Cresse in a house in Cambridge Road. January 1869 opened as an infants' school with 18 children, increasing to 46 in following year. School burned down March 5th 1873. 1875 new school (first building on the Cornwallis estate) built in 'Step Meadow', so called because of steps to it from Cambridge Road. Opposite school was a large watercress bed, and Braybrooke Road was a muddy lane known as 'the Gap'.

LONDON ROAD BOARD SCHOOL
See Tower Road School.

MERCATORIA SCHOOL
See St Leonards School

MOUNT PLEASANT SCHOOL; 1881-1952
Manor Road/Mount Pleasant Road.
Infants' opened in May 1881 by Hastings School Board, the building cost £1200, the land £2000. School for older boys and girls opened 15 January 1883 with 280 pupils, rising to 400 by 1884 and 600 later. May 1888 alterations and extension to boys' and girls' school completed. William Evans headmaster 1883-1916. Isabel Jukes headmistress 1883-1896. 1892 infants' school extended, playgrounds enlarged and separate entrances built for boys and girls. In total the school now provided places for 1000 pupils. A Laundry School and Handicraft Centre existed by 1918. On re-organisation in 1926, the Mount Pleasant Schools included Infants, Mixed Junior and Boys Senior. In 1952 became part

of Elphinstone Junior School. By 1958 and until 1978 the Handicraft Centre was an annex of Hastings Secondary Boys School. The original school buildings continued to be used until 1984, and in 1985 were demolished, the land being used for sheltered housing.

OPEN AIR SCHOOL
150 Athelstan Road.
A school in 1931.

ORE BOARD SCHOOL
See Sandown School.

ORE PLACE SCHOOL; 1871-1888
Ore Place.
Opened in an 'iron building' let to Ore School Board by a Mr Spalding (Vice-Chairman of the Board) for £1 per year. 1888 scholars transferred to schoolhouse adjoining St Helens Church. See St Helens School.

ORE RAGGED SCHOOL
Church Street.
Intended for those unable to pay for themselves. In 1871 maintained by a Miss St Paul.

ORE VILLAGE SCHOOL; 1851-
Old London Road.
On opening places for 120 boys, 100 girls and 100 infants. First headmaster Mr Hunter. Rebuilt 1855. 1886 W.F. Whitfield headmaster. 1888 Whitfield also Secretary of the Ore Friendly Society and the Ore Penny Dinner Fund. 1895 school enlarged to hold 250 boys, 158 girls and 150 infants. In c.1945 became Ore Secondary Modern School for Girls. Building is now the Ore Centre.

PARKERS SCHOOL
See Hastings Grammar School.

PRIORY ROAD SCHOOL; 1891-1944
Priory Road.
For origins see Bourne Walk School. Boys' school opened by Hastings School Board 18 September, on land at junction of Croft and Priory Roads. Intended to take the place of Bourne Walk School. The site cost £1200, the original building £2944. It was planned to add buildings for girls and infants. On re-organisation in 1926 became a selective central school taking boys and girls from the age of 11 instead of 7. 1944

became Hastings Secondary Modern School for Boys, with 427 on roll. 1956 with closure of Hastings Technical School and distribution of pupils among existing Secondary Modern Schools, became Hastings Secondary Boys' School. 1978 became part of the newly titled William Parker School. Priory Road buildings used as an annex to William Parker until 1982. 1890s building constructed for the original infants department today houses Hastings Teachers Centre.

RAGGED SCHOOL; 1855-
Stone Street.
School open in November.

ST ANDREWS SCHOOL; 1872-
Stonefield Road.
Opened 7 October with 43 boys. Site provided by Countess Waldegrave. By 1918 spaces for 90 boys, 130 girls and 96 infants. Average attedances were, respectively 79, 87, and 54. On post-war closure, building used as a carpet warehouse and later as a Greek Orthodox church although it is now empty.

ST CLEMENTS SCHOOL
Cavendish Terrace.
1871 an infants school.

ST HELENS SCHOOL; 1888-1911
The Ridge.
See Ore Place School. Original building next to St Helen's Church let to Ore School Board by the trustees of the late Rev. W.T. Turner. Transferred to Hastings School Board November 1897 (with extension of borough boundaries). New Mixed and Infants School opened 7 January 1901 on land bought for £510 from the Goodwin Trustees, the building, on The Ridge, costing £9755. 1906 unused portion of school became a girls' pupil teacher centre, although this was not recognised by the Board of Education in London. 1911 premises used to house the new Hastings Secondary School for Girls

ST LEONARDS SCHOOL; c.1834-present
Various locations.
Church of England National School, founded by Mrs James Burton with the first classes being held in the Assembly Rooms (now Masonic Hall) St Leonards. 1834 purpose built National School opened in St Clement's Place. 1847 new school built at a cost of £750 in Mercatoria

by Decimus Burton, for 189 boys, 189 girls and 182 infants. Joint salary of first headmaster and headmistress £75. This building survives, but the school has now moved to and become Collingwood School, Collingwood Drive.

ST LEONARDS BRITISH AND INFANTS SCHOOL
Gensing Station Road.
A school in 1871, closed by c.1895.

ST MARY IN THE CASTLE; 1830(?)-
Various locations.
A Church of England school started by the Rev. W. Wallinger for boys and girls in a loft near the Pelham Arcade. Purpose built school opened in (probably) 1834 for girls. In about 1835 boys moved to room over stables in Wellington Mews. New school buildings opened before 1840, and St Mary's became part of the National School system. Two additional sets of buildings put up in the 1840s. 1860 Drill Hall in Wellington Mews erected. 1877 Vores Memorial Hall opened, and used by the school for infant teaching (and also for parish meetings). 1896 new school completed—boys upstairs and girls downstairs, old girls' school buildings sold. 1932 a new (parish) hall built which also provided a roof-playground. As part of the re-organisation of education in Hastings, St Mary's lost the junior (7 to 11) pupils in 1926, although a new senior mixed school, the largest in the town with 9 classes, came into being. The Portland Place building is now used by Hastings Housing Department.

ST MARY MAGDALEN SCHOOL; 1856-
St John's Road/Magdalen Road.
Foundation stone laid December 17 1855, by Dowager Lady St John. Cost £2243. Originally a 'penny school', although pupils required to pay the considerable sum of sixpence a week. Later a boys school. The building is now used as private flats.

ST MARY STAR OF THE SEA SCHOOL; -present
Various locations.
A Catholic school originally in High Street. 1959 moved into the Sacred Heart Convent, Old London Road.

ST MATTHEW'S SCHOOL; -1943
Various locations.
Originally a day school in St Matthew's Church (in building that is now

the parish hall), subsequently in Grove Cottages. 1878 new schools at Strood Road opened by Thomas Brassey for 270 children—infants and girls—at a cost of £1600. Enlarged the following year and in 1900. Bombed in March 1943 and buildings later demolished. Site now occupied by private houses.

ST MICHAEL'S PAROCHIAL SCHOOL
Location unknown.
The Hastings and St Leonards News on 7th August 1868 recorded that T Barnes, the master for 30 years, was presented with a Bible. School may have been on the 'America Ground'—the seafront east of White Rock.

ST PAUL'S SCHOOL; 1871-present
Various locations.
Original National School building in St Pauls Road cost £2200, on land given by the 'Charity Trustees', for 150 boys and girls and 100 infants. Infants' school included soup kitchen and blanket store. In post-war period the school moved to Horntye Road, original building demolished and the site used by the YMCA.

SANDOWN INFANT SCHOOL; 1880-present
School Road.
Opened 12 January, on land sold by a Mr Goodwin, probably for £400. 1889 a Mixed School joined the Infants' on the same site. Moved to The Ridge in 1968.

SAUNDERS SCHOOL
See Hastings Grammar School.

SCHOOL OF COOKERY; 1890-
Mount Pleasant and Tower Road.
Opened 16 May under Miss Kate Sayles, for girls in the upper standards in voluntary and board schools.

SCHOOL OF ART AND SCIENCE
Brassey Institute, Claremont and at 42, George Street.

SILVERHILL SCHOOL; -c.1970
Paynton Road/Sedlescombe Road North.
1878 a new board school opened for 112 boys, 112 girls and 100 infants. 1883 enlarged for 120 additional pupils. Original buildings now demolished, flats erected on site, and school moved to Perth Road with

name changed to 'Silverdale'.

TOWER ROAD SCHOOL; 1896-
Tower Road.
Original pupils came from London Road Board Schools (which had been condemned). Site purchased from Magdalen Charity Trustees. 7 February 1899 Boys' School converted into a Mixed School, and the Girls' School into an Infants' School.

WEST ST LEONARDS SCHOOL; 1895-present
Bexhill Road/Filsham Road.
Also known as Bopeep School. A central hall and six classrooms for 400 pupils. Estimated cost of £4812 exceeded by c.£250 because of 'difficulties encountered in the special nature of the site'. Although designed as a boys' school, originally used as a mixed school. 1898 infants school opened by Hastings School Board at a cost of £3347 and for a maximum 294 children. Because of nature of the site 'a thick mass of concrete' necessary before building proper could start.

WATERLOO PLACE SCHOOL; 1885/6-
Waterloo Place
School building condemned in July 1889. In 1918 spaces for 213 infants, although average attendance was only 86. There were also spaces for 191 older girls (average attendance 126).

SOURCES AND BIBLIOGRAPHY

The research for this directory was carried out using the Hastings Reference Library local studies collection, including primary sources such as newspapers, street directories, and the records of local school boards and the education committee of the council. In addition, the following published books and pamphlets have been used:
M. Capon (1983) A Centenary Celebration of Mount Pleasant and Elphinstone Junior School, Hastings (Hastings).
C.C. Dobson (1934) The Story of St Mary in the Castle School Hastings (Hastings).
B. Funnell (1972) A History of Christ Church School, 1872-1972 (St Leonards-on-Sea).
Hastings Modern History Workshop (1983) The History of Ore to 1914. (Hastings).
B. Lawes (1987) Helenswood School and its Origins, 1870-1987

(Hastings).

J. Manwaring Baines (1956) History of Hastings Grammar School, 1619-1956 (Hastings, HGS Governors).

J. Manwaring Baines (1986) Historic Hastings, amended and revised edition (St Leonards-on-Sea, Cinque Port Press).

J. Manwaring Baines (undated) The Hastings Boys British School (Unpublished photocopy).